MW01631035
CITY OF CARLSBAD

2002 marks Carlsbad's 50th Anniversary! We are delighted to participate in the celebration of this occasion with the publication of this book highlighting the city's history. It is full of interesting information about the people and events that have shaped the development of this city. Many of the over two hundred photos it contains have never been published.

As you read this book, we hope you will gain a renewed appreciation for the people, forces and events that have been instrumental in creating the great city in which we live today.

We wish to thank Don Schemp, President of Capital Bank of North County, for his support of the publication of this book.

We are proud to present *WINDOWS ON THE PAST: An Illustrated History of Carlsbad, California* by Susan Gutierrez.

Claude "Bud" Lewis	Ann Kulchin	Ramona Finnila	Matt Hall	Julianne Nygaard
MAYOR	MAYOR PRO TEM	COUNCIL MEMBER	COUNCIL MEMBER	COUNCIL MEMBER

Rancho Santa Fe Bank (previously Capital Bank of North County) prides itself in being a community-oriented bank, working hard to make the communities we serve better places to live and work. It is with this spirit that we bring you this limited-edition book, a pictorial journey of Carlsbad, California . . . a city our bank has proudly served for over seventeen years.

We hope that through the reading of this book you will have renewed interest in the diverse group of people that make up this great city. We ask you to join with us in celebrating and valuing the lives and cultures of those individuals who contributed, and continue to contribute today, to the richness of the community of Carlsbad.

Don Schemp
PRESIDENT, CAPITAL BANK OF NORTH COUNTY

Dust jacket: *Aerial looking north towards the downtown of Carlsbad with San Diego Gas and Electric Company Encina Power Plant in foreground, circa 1985.*

End Sheet: *The current Carlsbad City Hall, circa 2002, was built on Pio Pico Drive in the late 1960s after Interstate 5 was widened and Pio Pico realigned.*

THE
DONNING COMPANY
PUBLISHERS

Windows on the Past

AN ILLUSTRATED HISTORY OF
CARLSBAD, CALIFORNIA

by Susan Schnebelen Gutierrez

For information write The Donning Company/Publishers, 184 Business Park Drive, Suite 206, Virginia Beach, VA 23462

Steve Mull, General Manager
Barbara Bolton, Project Director
Pam Forrester, Project Research Coordinator
Dawn V. Kofroth, Assistant General Manager
Richard A. Horwege, Senior Editor
Marshall McClure, Senior Graphic Designer
John Harrell, Imaging Artist
Scott Rule, Director of Marketing
Gigi Abbott, Marketing Assistant

Library of Congress Cataloging-in-Publication Data

Gutierrez, Susan Schnebelen, 1957–
Windows on the past : an illustrated history of Carlsbad, California / by Susan Schnebelen Gutierrez.
p. cm.
Includes bibliographical references (p.) and index.
ISBN 1-57864-164-0 (alk. paper)
1. Carlsbad (Calif.)—History. 2. Carlsbad (Calif.)—History—Pictorial works. I. Title.

F869.C26 .G88 2002
979.4'98—dc21

2002019221

Printed in the
United States of America

CONTENTS

CHAPTER 1

Early Influences

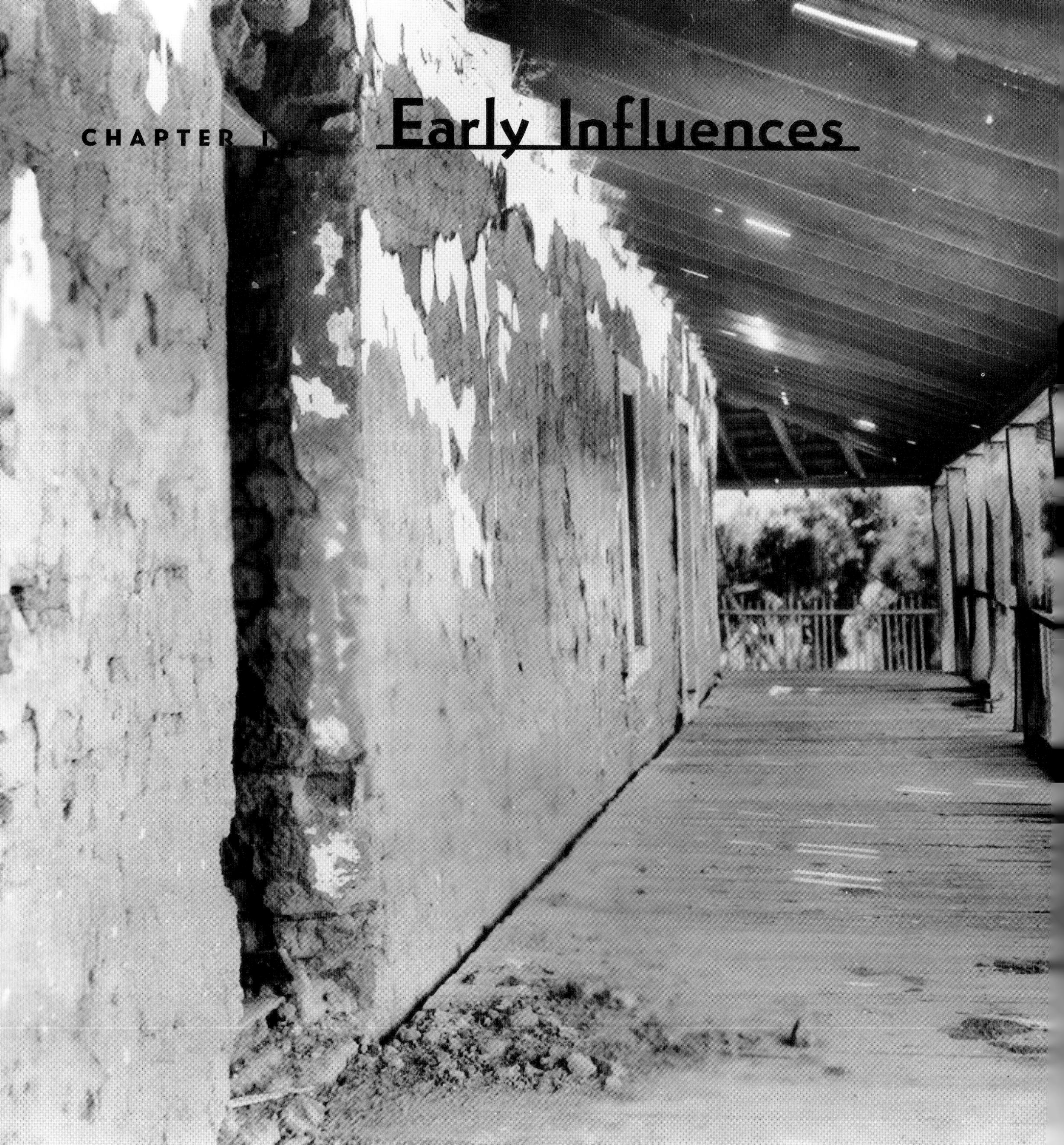

The Spanish Connection: Expeditions and Missions

Carlsbad's history is a combination of many separate influences. As each new group of people immigrated to the area, they added to the richly woven tapestry of Carlsbad's history. Written historical documentation of Carlsbad can be traced to Spain's 1769 Sacred Expedition led by the Franciscan Father Junípero Serra and Spanish Military Commander Gaspar de Portola. This was the first time that Spain authorized exploration of the California interior. Spain's colonization of the Americas began in 1492 with Columbus discovering the West Indies. In 1493, Pope Alexander VI's papal bull "Inter cetera divina" divided the New World discoveries between Spain and Portugal. One must remember that this was a pre-Reformation period and therefore European nations abided by Papal decisions. Pope Alexander VI's decision gave Spain permission to embark on three hundred years of exploration, conquest, and colonization in the Americas. The only contact between California and Spain during this time occurred when Juan Rodriguez Cabrillo led a brief exploratory mission in 1542. He landed in San Diego as well as a few other sites. Spain for all practical purposes forgot California for over two hundred years, concentrating on their more lucrative holdings in Mexico and Perú. The silver and gold mine yield from both of those countries occupied Spain's interest and boosted their economy while causing hyperinflation throughout the rest of Europe.

Rancho Agua Hedionda Adobe, circa 1930, was later known as the Kelly Ranch. (Courtesy of San Diego Historical Society)

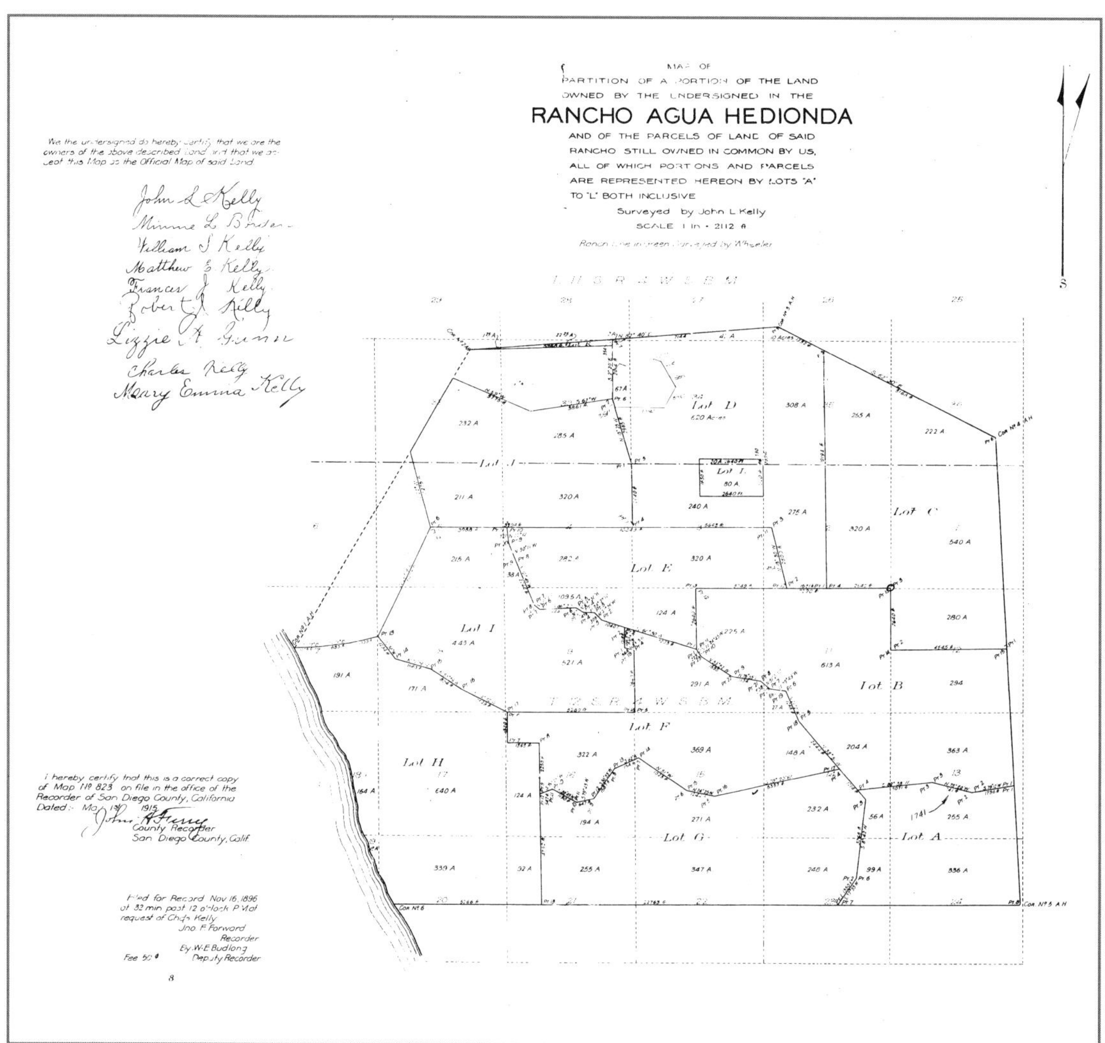

Rancho Agua Hedionda.

After the Reformation, a few European nations gradually challenged Spain's hold on their outlying American territories. After 1620, England began serious colonization of the Eastern Americas, in what are now New England and Virginia. By 1769, England was more willing to challenge Spain and ventured into the Caribbean and as far as the California coast. Russian interest in the Pacific Northwest of the Americas combined with English attention to the area, spurred Spain into launching the Sacred Expedition to claim ownership of this vast unknown territory.

Spain's preferred method of colonization always entailed using the combined forces of church and military. They believed that it was their obligation to convert all unbaptised heathens to Catholicism as repayment for God's grace in allowing them to defeat the Moors in 1492 and finally ending Arab occupation of Spain. Because of Spanish beliefs, the military and the church led all Sacred Expeditions equally, each concerned with their own area of expertise. The primary objective of this 1769 Sacred Expedition was to map geographic areas and discover appropriate establishment sites for towns and missions based on the locations and quantities of natives. Once the expedition arrived in the San Diego Region, Father Serra decided to remain there for a time, leaving Father Crespi to accompany Portola overland. From their journals we find the first written accounts of Carlsbad. Their journals describe traveling over a good road that would later become the genesis of El Camino Real, and of meeting up with various native peoples who lived around the lagoons. The soldiers who accompanied the expedition named the lagoon *Agua Hedionda*, meaning "stinky water." However, Father Crespi recorded it as San Simeón Lipmaca, and he listed Buena Vista Lagoon as Santa Sinforosa.

In 1798 Father Lausen established the Mission San Luis Rey de Francia. At this time the Carlsbad area, which was part of the mission landholdings, fully felt the impact of Spain's domination and control. Establishment of a mission involved more than

Kelly Valley looking southwest from Calavera towards El Camino Real, circa 1920.

LAND GRANTS

Rancho Agua Hedionda, originally called Rancho San Francisco, was a thirteen-thousand-acre grant issued to Juan María Romouldo Marrón of San Diego in 1842 by Governor Juan Batista Alvarado. It is this block of land that eventually provided the foundation of present-day Carlsbad. A small section of the land grant, Rancho Los Encinitas, issued in 1842 to Don Andrés Ybarra, also became part of Carlsbad. The remnants of Don Ybarra's adobe ranch house are located at Stagecoach Park in Carlsbad's southeast quadrant.

building a church. Missions were self-sufficient entities that combined religious conversion of the native peoples along with development of cattle ranches, orchards, and water systems. They were very much like small towns. The religious leaders who ran the missions were responsible for the physical as well as the spiritual well-being of the natives under their control.

Though relatively short-lived, lasting only about thirty years in the Carlsbad area, the Mission San Luis Rey's impact was significant: displacing natives from their homes and changing their cultural, social, and religious practices. The mission also introduced new agricultural methods as well as nonnative plant materials and, most importantly, originated the concept of private land ownership.

Each mission had specific boundaries within which the mission fathers made and enforced all decisions based on the needs of those living under their jurisdiction.

The Mexican Influence and Rancho Agua Hedionda

By 1821, Mexico gained independence from Spain, and the mission period soon ended. Division and secularization of the rich mission lands occurred throughout California. By 1834, Mexican Governor Alvarado was issuing the first private land grants from the partitioned mission lands. Mission San Luis Rey was divided into five separate land grants: Aqua Hedionda, Buena Vista, Encinitas, Guajome, and Los Vallecitos de San Marcos. It must be remembered that not all the former mission lands were included in land grants; some was left vacant, providing free range between the private landholdings.

Americanization

In 1846, America fulfilled its Manifest Destiny when it entered into a war with Mexico known as the Mexican War. By 1848, the war had ended with Mexico losing almost one-half of its total territory to the United States. After a brief twenty-one-year period, Mexican rule over California ended. In the Treaty of Guadalupe Hidalgo, signed by the United States and Mexico 1848, the same rights were guaranteed to Mexican citizens living in the newly acquired U.S. territories as if they were already U.S. citizens.

While recognition of property ownership was assured in the treaty, it was sometimes difficult to maintain. A variety of reasons were at fault; one difference was as simple as legal property description. When mission land was partitioned and Mexican land grants were issued, property descriptions were based on the location of natural features such as trees, streams, or hills. *Diseños* or drawings depicting these features were considered adequate as property descriptions. The United States based property titles on accurate surveys. In fact one of the first things the U.S. government did at the conclusion of the Mexican War was to send out survey teams that documented accurate boundary lines and grids throughout the Southwest.

Additional problems encountered in retaining property title were debts and how they were paid off. Under Mexican practice, a gentleman's agreement was reached and negotiated and hands were shaken: the deal was done. U.S. law had papers signed, liens issued, and property confiscated if loans were not repaid.

Immediately after the war a flood of Americans arrived in California, mainly heading for the Northern California gold fields. Those that came and settled in Southern California did so for ranching and farming. Settling on the ranches with their families, they intended to live there year round, unlike their California counterparts who lived in town as well as on their ranchos.

Juan María Romouldo Marrón died in 1853 while California was undergoing drastic changes. In his will the grantee, Juan María Romouldo Marrón, left 362 acres on the northern border of his Rancho Agua Hedionda, the area known as Rinconada de Buena Vista y El Salto, to his younger brother and godson Sylvester Marrón, along with grazing rights on the entire Rancho property. The remaining 12,000 acres of Rancho Agua Hedionda and a second Ranch in Baja California, Rancho Los Cuervos de Vernado, were left to his wife Felipa and four surviving children: María de la Luz, José Cayetano, Juan Nepomuceno, and Ignacio de Jesús (Carron, October 2001). In the years immediately after Juan María Romouldo's death, his family entered into a series of leases on Rancho Agua Hedionda. In 1860 Felipa Marrón entered into an agreement with Francis J. Hinton, exchanging money for use of Rancho Agua Hedionda. Five years later in 1865 property title was transferred to Hinton.

The Kellys and Other Early Settlers

Francis Hinton hired Robert Kelly, an émigré from the Isle of Man (Mann), to oversee operations on Rancho Agua Hedionda. Kelly, who moved into an adobe home built originally by the Marrón family near the Agua Hedionda Creek, was well suited for the job. He had previously co-owned and run a ranch in Jamacha, owned and operated a mercantile in San Diego, and served in the U.S. Army postwar Survey Commission. By 1868 Robert's older brother Matthew arrived in the area with his wife and family to establish a ten-thousand-acre homestead, named "Los Kiotes," southeast of the Rancho Agua Hedionda's southernmost border. Francis Hinton's death in 1870 left Robert Kelly as sole inheritor and owner of Rancho Agua Hedionda. A succession of lawsuits from long lost Hinton relatives and Marrón family members raised objections to Kelly's inheritance. When all legal issues were resolved, Kelly retained title to Rancho Agua Hedionda, Hinton relatives inherited property in other locations, and the Sylvester Marrón family accepted ownership of the 362 acres known as Rinconada de Buena Vista, located on the northern fringe of the Rancho land grant.

In 1880, Robert Kelly granted a coastal right of way to the Southern California Railway, providing the connection between San Diego and points north. The connection of rail lines spurred development of previously never owned or developed coastal land. One rail stop was just northwest of Rancho Agua Hedionda and would shortly become known as Frazier's Station. The other stop, southwest of the land grant, was known as Stewart's Station. The Hayes and Hicks Inland Mail and Stage Company, a flourishing stagecoach business, ran daily stages between the inland towns of Escondido, San Marcos (or Barnham), and Fallbrook and the coastal rail lines.

John Frazier and family were among the first to arrive by train in 1883 and they settled on 160 acres close to the ocean west of the rail lines, just south of Buena Vista Lagoon. Frazier's various occupations, such as mining, farming, and life onboard a ship prepared him for the difficulties in this new settlement. Lack of potable water was a major hindrance to any farming efforts. The land was rather worthless if it did not have a water source. Most farmers in the area tried digging wells since the nearby lagoons usually dried up during the summers. To guarantee clean fresh water, families collected rain that ran off roofs into cisterns or brought water by horse and wagon from the closest fresh water source, the El Salto Falls at Marrón Gorge, about four miles away. Considering that horse and wagon undertook this trek, water was a very precious commodity, and not used lightly.

Frazier decided that there had to be a better and easier way to provide water for his family and his farm. Frazier contracted the Mull Brothers, expert well borers, to dig a well. The

Oceanside newspaper, *The Wavelets*, reported that John Frazier agreed to pay $3.00 per drilled foot, not to exceed 600 feet, to find water. One can imagine his relief in 1885, when water was discovered at 245 feet. Eventually, both mineral and artesian water were discovered and excitedly reported in the local newspapers. Overnight the discovery of water so near the coastline increased the value of land by 50 percent. Frazier built a platform near the rail line and began offering train passengers water. His fame grew and the area near his home and wells was known as Frazier's Station.

Marrón Gorge pond off of Haymar Road was one source of pre-1880 water supply for early Carlsbad residents.

By the 1880s the American populace had recovered from the devastation of the Civil War and was looking for new opportunities. Completion of the transcontinental railroad, rail lines running throughout California, and cheap train fares from the Midwest to the Pacific all contributed to a population in motion. A land boom was underway and many had just one destination in mind, the West.

CHAPTER 2

The 1880s and '90s: Water, Religion, and New Commerce

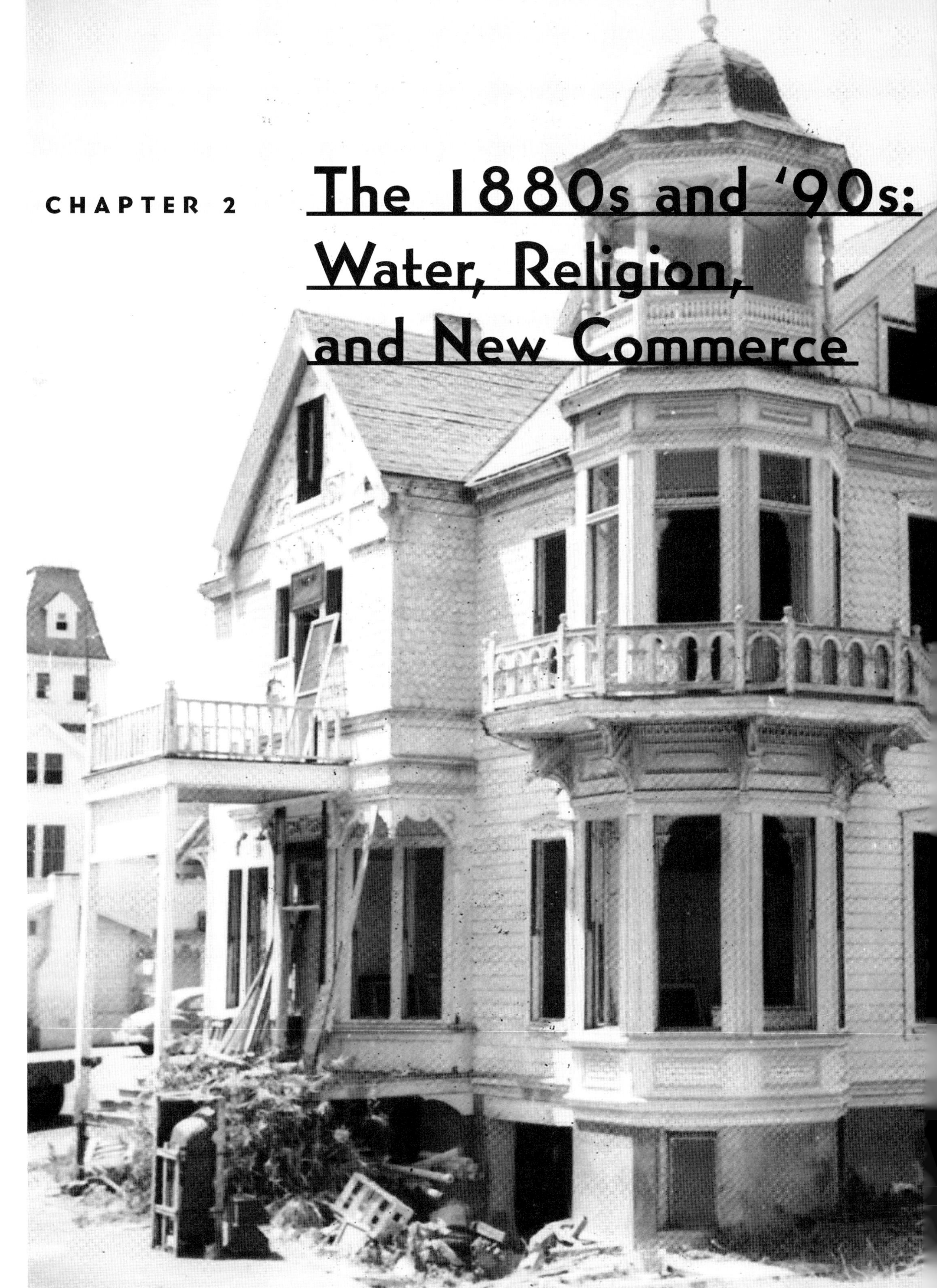

Civil War veteran Gerhard Schutte and his friend D. D. Wadsworth were looking for possible investment opportunities. Hearing of Frazier's Station and the well water that showed a water analysis indicating a similarity to that of the famous Well Number Nine in the Karlsbad Bohemia Spas, they decided to investigate. After gathering favorable information in 1886, Schutte, Wadsworth, and two other investors, Samuel Church Smith and Henry Nelson, formed a real estate investment group that they called Carlsbad Land and Water Company. Carlsbad, the anglicized version of Karlsbad, was chosen to emphasize the connection with the famed spa. The company purchased 270 acres from Frazier and 130 adjoining acres of coastal land at $40 an acre. These 400 acres were entirely outside of the Kelly Rancho Agua Hedionda land grant and the Marron property of Rinconada de Buena Vista. The Carlsbad Land and Water Company set about forming a town. John Frazier was retained as general superintendent of the wells, since the availability of water was an important selling point for any Western lands. Additional wells were sunk and water was piped throughout the newly formed town. The town was called Carlsbad in the promotional advertisements rather than Rancho Agua Hedionda or Frazier's Station, creating an identity apart from a Rancho or railway stop. The Carlsbad Land and Water Company paid for advertisements throughout the United States and Europe.

Wadsworth House was built by Carlsbad Land and Water Company Vice President D. D. Wadsworth.

The Carlsbad Land and Water Company laid out the town in grids with numbered streets running west to east from the rail lines. What we currently refer to as State Street was then called First, followed by Second through Fifth. The streets were demarcated with trees, most often eucalyptus. The company invested a substantial amount of money into the new venture. Several homes built by company founders remain today. The homes that were built were very different from the adobe structures common to the area, emphasizing a Midwest rather than a Spanish or Mexican flavor, making it seem a bit more comfortable and homelike to new investors. The Schutte Home on Carlsbad Boulevard, now known as Neiman's Restaurant, was built in a Victorian theme, and the Smith Home, now located on Beech Avenue in Magee Park, was a typical Midwest house that included a snow porch.

Schutte Home / Twin Inns/ Neiman's Restaurant was built by Carlsbad Land and Water Company President Gerhard Schutte.

In 1887, one year after the formation of the Carlsbad Land and Water Company, the population of Carlsbad was three hundred. Promotional literature such as the *Golden Era* published an article that year stating, "Carlsbad is destined to occupy a foremost place among the great sanitariums of the world." The company invested $50,000, a huge sum of money at that time, to build the Carlsbad Hotel, which was destroyed by fire shortly after it opened in 1896. Actually, by the time of the fire, land sales in Carlsbad had practically ceased and several company founders such as Samuel Church Smith had moved to more profitable locations such as San Diego.

The 1890s decade was one of terrible drought. The population in Carlsbad dropped to 155, almost half the number from just three years before. A general slowdown

Magee House was built by Carlsbad Land and Water Company secretary Samuel Church Smith.

in Carlsbad's growth occurred as the combined forces of drought and national economic depression affected the city. Carlsbad now entered into a twenty-four-year period of slow to no growth. Things became so precarious that the school, where enrollment had been growing by leaps and bounds just a few years before, was in actual danger of closing for lack of pupils. At times there were less than five students attending. Most of the city was abandoned and had only six registered voters. The outlying ranches with the Bordon, Kelly, and Marron families kept the area populated. The Schutte family remained in town as one of the original Land Company families. Gerhard Schutte stayed in Carlsbad until 1906, when he moved to National City with his wife Bertha. Several of his children married into other Carlsbad families, such as the Reeses, Kruetzcamps, and Carpenters. Frazier had moved to Los Angeles and died in 1890. Basically the city was deserted.

One of the few positive additions to the town during the 1890s was the establishment of St. Michael's Episcopal Church by Father Jacobs. As a result of the advertisement campaign in England that promoted the new American West, many English citizens formed expatriate communities in San Luis Rey, Carlsbad, and Encinitas. Episcopal missionary priests established small missions in their communities and also served in a small

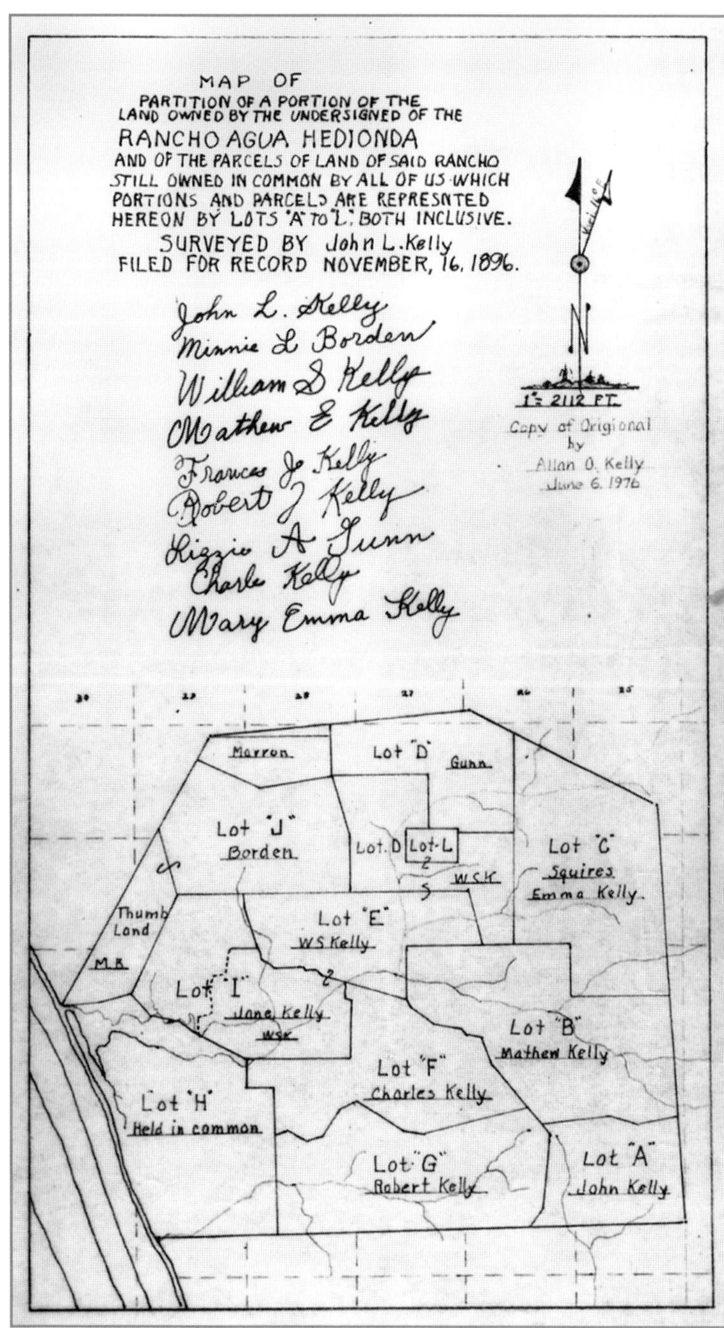

Map of Partition of Rancho Agua Hedionda.

church located on Carlsbad Boulevard and Lincoln. The Ramsays, Shipleys, and the Shaws were all founding members of St. Michael's Church. They provided money, labor, and land in order to build the parish. In 1959 the Old St. Michael's Church moved to Carlsbad Boulevard and Christiansen Way.

While the Carlsbad Land and Water Company was forming in the current northwest quadrant of the city, a similar enterprise was occurring in the coastal area just south of the Rancho Agua Hedionda borders. In 1886, Thomas E. Metcalf, one of the La Costa Land and Town Company founders, along with his brother Alfred and Jacob Gruendike, purchased land from Oliver H. Bordon, father of W. W. Bordon who published and edited the *Plain Truth* newspaper. O. H. Borden, who settled in the Batiquitos area in 1874, sold all 550 acres of land in "his upper and lower places" as reported in the *Plain Truth*, to the La Costa Land Company for $18 to $20 an acre. Additionally, the La Costa Land and Town Company purchased 160 acres at $25 an acre from J. C. Peterson. The total 710 acres for the proposed town included land from the present-day La Costa Resort to the Pacific Ocean and on both sides of the Batiquitos Lagoon. But this endeavor along the coast was doomed to failure. The land lacked an adequate water supply. The coastal area around Batiquitos Lagoon, while never part of any rancho land grant or developed town, was destined to remain a rather sparsely populated area until development of the La Costa Resort in the 1960s.

Robert Kelly died in 1890 willing his property, the Rancho Agua Hedionda land grant directly east of the fledgling town of Carlsbad, to his brother Matthew's nine children. Between the years 1892 and 1896 the entire land grant was held in common, except for a section in the northwest section sold in 1893 to a

Mr. Thorpe. The sale was necessary, bringing needed cash into the family and ensuring their survival during the drought years. Shortly after the property was sold, Mr. Thorpe resold the land to the Thum Brothers, who held the patent on the Tanglefoot Fly Paper. The land became known as Thum Lands.

After the Rancho property was surveyed and divided into equitable parcels based on availability of grazing and water, each section was assigned an alphabetical letter. The letter was then placed on a slip of paper and as each heir drew his or her slip the ownership of that parcel was transferred. Minnie Kelly Borden gave up her rights to draw from the slips of paper, in order to choose a preferred section of land, and two parcels were held in common. While the drought continued, a few of the Kelly heirs began homesteading land that adjoined their parcels to support their grazing livestock.

During the decade of drought that followed Robert Kelly's death, ranching and dry farming of beans, corn, and hay became the only agricultural options. A few other enterprises undertaken were prospecting for oil and copper mining. While ranching was difficult during the dry years, the ranch families were in a better position regarding water than those that lived in town, since many of them lived near creeks or had already dug wells. For those who remained in town, digging a well meant the well level would be precariously close to the water level of their outhouses.

Kelly family at Rancho Agua Hedionda.

CHAPTER 3

The Early 1900s: Agriculture and Land Development

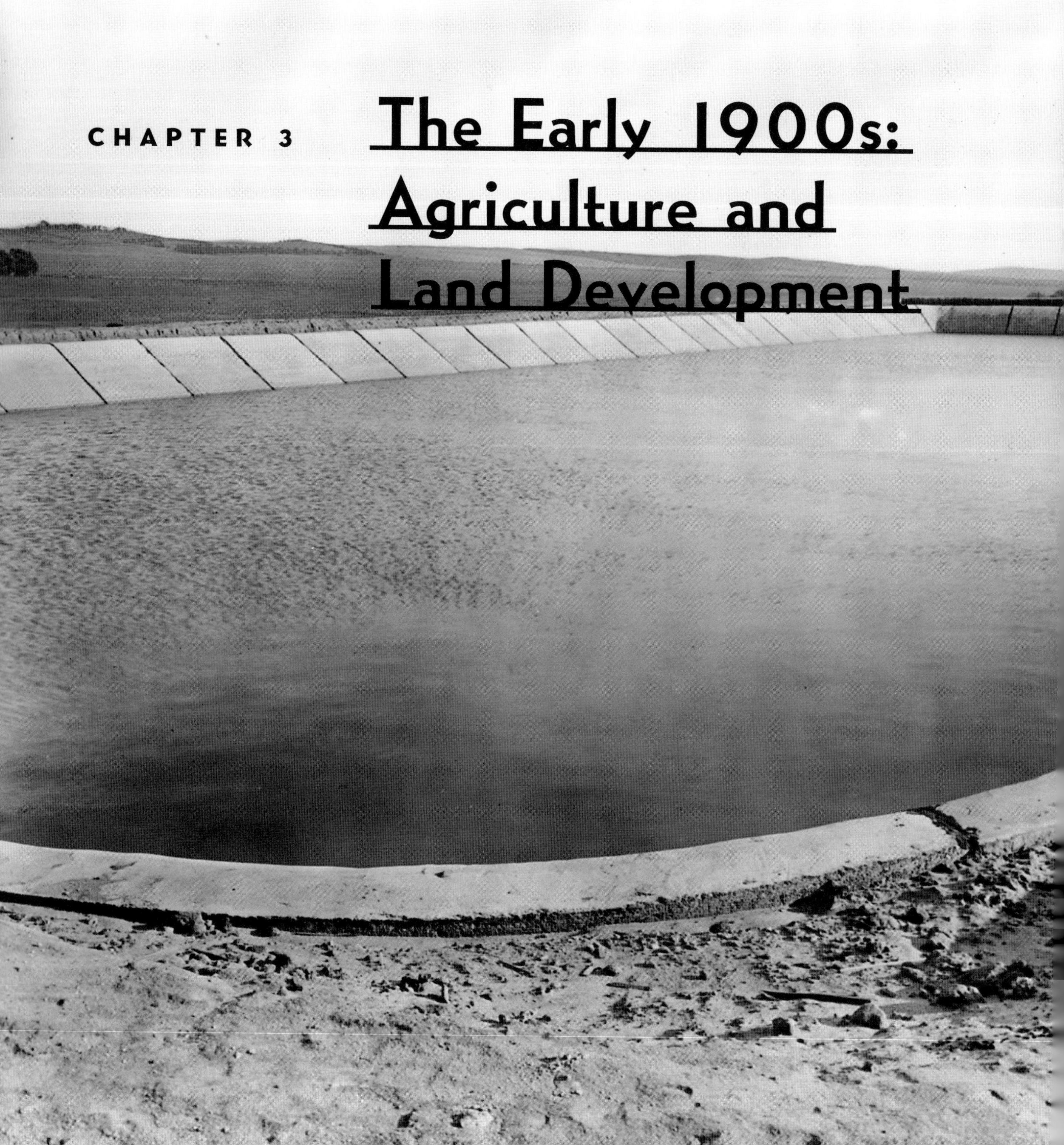

For those families remaining in Carlsbad, water continued to be an important issue. Many of them were dependent on the mineral well that Frazier had opened in 1884. In 1906 W. W. Borden reported in the newspaper the *Spirit of Love* that the waterworks ceased to function, and that Mr. Shipley, who had purchased the Samuel Church Smith home in 1896, paid to put the waterworks in order.

Gerhard Schutte sold his home on Carlsbad Boulevard to the South Coast Land Company in 1906, and they immediately began using it as housing for their company employees. H. C. Young, a South Coast employee moved into the Schutte home and lived there until 1913 while he worked laying six-inch waterline pipes. In 1913 the South Coast Land Company signed an agreement that guaranteed water delivery from the San Luis Rey Valley to Carlsbad within one year. The water would run in pipes across the Buena Vista lagoon. By 1914 the South Coast Land Company had purchased all the remaining Carlsbad Land and Water Company land and drilled six water wells in the San Luis Rey Valley. Running the lines to Carlsbad infused the town with new life.

Reservoir constructed in 1919 looking south from Carlsbad's northern boundary. (Courtesy of San Diego Historical Society)

Los Diego Hotel and Armstrong and Newcomb Real Estate Office on Grand and State, circa 1920s.

With an adequate source of water there was no stopping the influx of people, particularly farmers. The first avocado grove, begun by Sam Thompson in 1916, was followed by many more. Avocado groves spawned an entirely new industry for Carlsbad. In 1922 the avocado growers began an annual Avocado Day Festival downtown to introduce the public to the many ways one could prepare the fruit. By 1928 Carlsbad promoted itself as the "Home of the Avocado," with seven thousand people attending Avocado Day celebrations. The South Coast Land Company took advantage of this opportunity and began selling five-acre lots of "avocado" land. In addition to the avocado groves that dotted the landscape, flower fields and subtropical fruits were introduced to the area.

In 1919 the growth potential was so positive that hardworking people, such as Eddie and Neva Kentner, risked leaving secure employment in order to move their family to Carlsbad and take over operation of the Twin Inns Restaurant. The Kentners first discovered Carlsbad when they visited Neva's sister Fern, who was married at the time to the Carlsbad railroad stationmaster. Fern later remarried and became Fern Chase.

This second attempt at developing Carlsbad, undertaken by the South Coast Land Company, was the one that stuck. By selling land in larger parcels it facilitated Carlsbad's development on a more solid foundation of agriculture. For each acre of land purchased, the company offered one share of water stock in the Oceanside Mutual Water Company, or one could purchase additional water stock as necessary. This was the water from the San Luis Rey Valley wells. The Oceanside Mutual Water Company became the Carlsbad Mutual Water Company, and by 1927 they owned and operated twenty-five miles of water transmission mains and distribution lines, as well as storage facilities and pumping plants. It was this stockholder-owned Water Company that provided Carlsbad with water until the 1950s, when the combined effects of increased population and water salinity forced the residents to look for another water source.

Many of the support businesses needed by the farmers, such as building supplies, small hotels, blacksmiths, and mercantilists congregated near the rail lines creating a solid downtown business district. State Street, where most of the businesses were located, had the distinction of being one of only two paved streets in town, an honor it held with Lincoln that ran parallel to the coast. Most of the other roads remained unpaved and were known as "Corduroy roads," a name derived from the street grading done by tractors, which left them rippled.

Left: Avocado Day Festival, looking north on State Street, circa 1925. (Courtesy San Diego Historical Society)

Top: Avocado Day Festival on State Street, circa 1925. (Courtesy San Diego Historical Society)

CHAPTER 4

The 1920s: Building Infrastructure for a New Town

Aerial looking west, circa 1927. (Courtesy San Diego Historical Society)

It was during the late teens and early twenties that most of the groundwork and infrastructure of community awareness was built. A sense of unity developed among the growing population as churches, theaters, hotels, and newspapers all established footholds in the community. Neighbors pulled together to face adversity as well as to build something new and beneficial. This realization that together they could build something important laid the groundwork for city incorporation thirty years later.

In 1922, Sally Troutman and her friend Marion Holmes started the first children's Sunday school in town. By 1924 the Sunday school had given birth to the Carlsbad Union Church, a denomination of the Conservative Congregational Christian Conference. Much of Carlsbad's nascent social and cultural life revolved around the Union Church activities. Their church slogan adopted in 1920, "In the Heart of the Community with the Community at Heart," is still in use today and emphasized the commingling of church and community activities prevalent from the very beginning of the church's establishment.

Wesleyan Methodist missionaries James and Marjorie Spencer arrived in Carlsbad in 1924 to establish a small mission church. Located south of Elm Avenue, the Spencers moved to the heart of the newly built Mexican neighborhood. The residents knew this area of Carlsbad as Barrio Carlos, most of whom had recently arrived to work in the agricultural fields and groves. A gentleman by the name of La Betta constructed small wooden homes to house the immigrants. These houses that were purchased for $500 were paid off in monthly installments and provided the foundation for Carlsbad's first neighborhood subdivision. In 1927 the Reverend John Henley, his wife Ruth, and son John arrived in town to continue the Mission work and relieve the Spencers, who were off to South America. The Henleys remained within Barrio Carlos working and raising their family until the 1950s. Reverend Henley was totally devoted to his missionary flock, even working in the flower fields as a majordomo for the Frazees.

Members of Reverend Henley's church remember his sermons and admonishments about attending the Carlsbad Theater located on State Street that opened in 1927. Carlsbad builders Chester Craig, F. H. Tolle, H. E. Fleisher, R. G. Chase, and Robert Baird financed the $40,000 construction. The theater opened in February 1927 with the silent movie *It* starring Clara Bow, billed as the "It Girl." Many critics viewed the theater as too grand for small town Carlsbad. The interior was decorated in ten- to fifteen-foot-high murals painted by a one-armed Scotsman, Alexander William MacRae. The murals had themes that depicted Carlsbad and the surrounding areas done in tones of soft greens, misty violets, clear blues, and dashes of sunsets. Places that were immortalized in the murals were San Luis Rey Mission; Lakes Hodges and Henshaw; Oceanside Pier; a Carlsbad collage of avocados, bulb gardens, and greenhouses; and Encinitas.

A large enough Catholic population lived in Carlsbad by 1924 to warrant establishment of Saint Patrick's Mission Church, administered by the Franciscan

Advent Christian Church Camp south of Buena Vista Lagoon, circa 1930s.

Aerial looking east, State Street in foreground, circa 1927. (Courtesy San Diego Historical Society)

fathers of Mission San Luis Rey. The first Sunday Mass celebrated in Carlsbad was in the Craig Store on Grand Avenue. Mr. and Mrs. Charles Krueztkamp donated land on Harding and Oak for the building of a permanent church in 1927. The Santa Fe Railroad supplied the church bell and Mr. and Mrs. Albert Cohn donated money towards the altar. Building funds were procured through the Catholic Church Extension Fund in Chicago. Separation from San Luis Rey Mission was finalized in 1943. New church buildings were constructed in 1950 on Harding Street and again in 1983 on Tamarack and Adams to accommodate the increase in church population.

The Adventist Christian Church bought six building lots in the subdivision of Granville Park, which was located just south of the Buena Vista Lagoon and west of the railroad tracks. Granville Park, originally planned in 1922 as a subdivision, was never quite able to develop into the planned neighborhood. The Adventist Church established annual summer camps on their

Road into Adventist Camp looking east towards Buena Vista Lagoon.

property. At times the weekend attendance would reach as high as five hundred people.

One of the most significant community events in the 1920s was establishment of the local weekly newspaper, the *Carlsbad Champion*, in 1925. Begun by William Maxwell, the *Champion* filled the gap left in reporting community events when W. W. Borden's *Spirit of Love* newspaper closed in 1924. Borden, who started his publishing career in 1882 with the first issue of *Our Paper*, printed in Barham, later known as San Marcos, covered a wide circulation area that included news from Escondido to the coast. Once Bordon began printing the *Spirit of Love* in 1900 from his Harding Street shop, he focused more intently on Carlsbad.

Following Borden's example, Maxwell adopted the *Spirit of Love* slogan "Independent but not Neutral" for the *Champion*. While continuing in Borden's footsteps, the *Champion* provided an invaluable service to Carlsbad residents, informing them of local as well as national news and thus providing a link to the outside world. It was the *Champion*, later known as the *Carlsbad Journal*, which linked the residents and gave them a sense of place and community. The newspaper recorded all items of interest, such as births, marriages, deaths, who was growing what and how much it was selling for, where people were going on vacation, what the Chamber of Commerce was up to, as well as the local schools and churches. The paper also informed and helped to rally the citizenry to local causes when necessary. For the next seventy years the newspaper recorded almost all the events in town, becoming the de facto recordkeepers and historians for Carlsbad.

Carlsbad continued its steady growth pattern throughout the 1920s. Constant improvements were undertaken, upgrading the conditions of the downtown area. In hopes of enticing new business to town, lateral sewage lines were laid in addition to the construction of a sewage treatment plant. When the town suffered a devastating fire in 1927 that wiped out six businesses and damaged many others at a cost of $40,000, the town and the residents sprung back and rebuilt. On the night of April 8, 1929, a fire started on State Street in the Carlsbad Sweet Shop, located in the wooden Killian Building. Six businesses were destroyed because there was no local fire service, no nearby water mains, and no fire hydrants. Within a week, plans were underway to reconstruct the Killian Building, this time in brick, and to relocate the businesses destroyed. Other shop owners in town undertook a collection to pay Oceanside firefighters who responded that night. They even remembered to collect an additional $30 as a donation for the local Boy Scout troop under the guidance and leadership of Scout Master Dewey McClellan, who showed up the night of the fire and relocated all the Drug Store's goods out of harm's way and guarded the bank.

Adventist Camp looking east at train tracks.

Below: Adventist Camp, Granville Park, looking west to Ocean.

Corner of State Street and Elm Avenue, circa 1930.

Not much seemed to keep Carlsbad residents down, not even when the stock market crashed in 1929. Construction of the California Carlsbad Mineral Spring Hotel continued and it opened with great fanfare in 1930. Capitalizing on the mineral well fame, the Eastman Hotel Company constructed a lavish hotel on Carlsbad Boulevard. The hotel offered a health clinic that included mineral baths as well as exercise classes broadcast on radio station KNX Los Angeles led by Dr. P. M. Seixas. Besides the health-related services, the hotel provided their guests with all manner of comforts, lavish restaurants, ballrooms, and sun parlors. All brought a touch of elegance to small town Carlsbad.

Directly across the street from the California Carlsbad Mineral Spring Hotel, C. O. Williams constructed an eighteen-hole minia-

Twin Inns on Carlsbad Boulevard, circa 1930.

ture golf course that also opened in 1930. The entire project was illuminated at night and the landscaped grounds housed a clubhouse with an Egyptian canopy. A running brook with waterfalls passed through the golf course fed from an artesian well. The landscaping consisted of a combination of Monterey cypress, palms, ferns, flowering moss, and roses planted throughout the golf course. It was billed as the second largest course in the state of California.

Top: South side of Elm Avenue looking east, 1930s.

Bottom: Looking north on State Street from Elm Avenue.

CHAPTER 5

The 1930s: The Depression and Its Following Downs and Ups

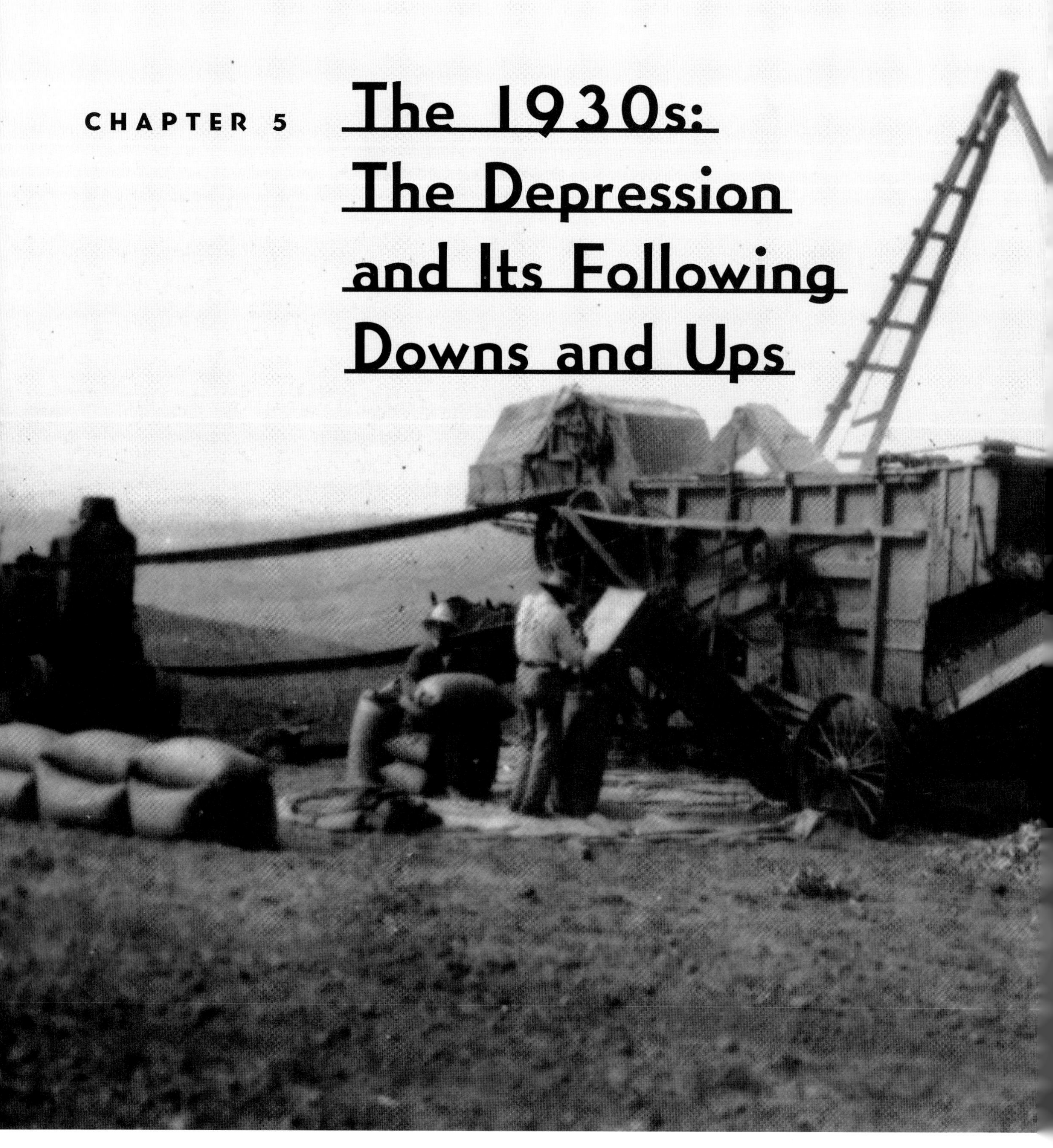

Even with all the new businesses in town, Carlsbad was not able to totally elude the effects of the national Depression. The city itself entered into another slow growth period. The First National Bank on Elm Avenue, that had just opened in the late 1920s, closed its doors or, as was commonly noted, went on a "Bank Holiday." Gradually, throughout the 1930s, the bank repaid investors in small increments the money they had deposited before the Depression. Some Carlsbad adults recall playing in the abandoned bank as children. It was a place furnished with piles of newspapers and an empty vault. Other adults remember their sorrow at seeing classmates living in the abandoned bank building with their families. Those families that were totally without any other resource were often forced into dividing the space behind the tellers' windows for living space. Albert Cohn, a wealthy Los Angeles grocer, who retired to Carlsbad and lived in a beautiful Spanish-style estate, donated many pairs of shoes to needy children in Carlsbad.

Hay baling on Rancho Agua Hedionda.

Kelly land looking northeast.

Regardless of the hardships suffered throughout town, Carlsbad hung on during the Depression. Perhaps not growing as fast as before 1929 or as prosperous, but it grew. A few of the weekend avocado growers, those who bought land on a whim while attending an Avocado Day Festival, didn't survive the Depression years. Many speculated that they would not have survived as avocado farmers even if the Depression had never occurred, since they lacked practical farming experience. During the halcyon days of the 1920s when Carlsbad was billed as "Home of the Avocado," many investors were thrilled with the notion of buying "Avocado Acres." They dreamed of retiring and becoming wealthy gentleman farmers, but it was this group that didn't survive. Those farmers and ranchers with real agricultural experience made it through the Depression, living off their land. Considering that for five years

Hay harvesting on Rancho Agua Hedionda.

Cattle branding on Rancho Agua Hedionda.

Carlsbad endured a severe drought, this was a significant achievement.

In 1933 the Works Progress Administration (WPA) or Public Works Administration (PWA) paid one hundred men sixty cents an hour to build a drainage system in Carlsbad. The Carlsbad Mutual Water Company also offered work when it began consecution of Calaveras Dam.

It is interesting to note that, in the midst of the Depression, the Carlsbad Planning Association, a scaled down version of the Carlsbad Chamber of Commerce, petitioned the San Diego County Board of Supervisors to adopt zoning ordinances for Carlsbad. This made Carlsbad the third town in San Diego County after Del Mar and Rancho Santa Fe to institute building restrictions. Edgar Hastings, chairman of the San Diego County Board of Supervisors, commented, "This will mean much to the future of Carlsbad. Instead of just growing with no restrictions or limitations, Carlsbad will take its place in orderly construction." (*Carlsbad Journal*, December 26, 1935)

In fact, it was during this period that Eddie Kentner enlarged his Twin Inns Restaurant, by adding a rear dining room. This room also had the famous canvas murals painted by J. Morton Patterson with the assistance of Edna Knox. These murals depicted San Diego backcountry landscapes such as Warner Hot Springs, Pala, and Julian.

By the late 1930s the Depression's grip loosened on Carlsbad and the city started to grow again. Eddie Kentner continued with his remodeling plans at the Twin Inns, adding new doors, fireplaces, kitchens, and powder rooms. A businessman does not undertake such extensive work if the business is not prosperous and growing.

One of the most significant events for Carlsbad during the

Depression was the 1936 relocation of the Davis Military Academy from Pacific Beach. Bringing needed cash to the city, it helped to relieve some of the impact of the Depression. Occupying the empty Red Apple Inn and surrounding property on Carlsbad Boulevard, the Davis Military Academy changed not only the school's address but also its name to the Army and Navy Academy.

Facing page: Twin Inns after dining room renovations.

In 1939 the Carlsbad Woman's Club asked Julia Shipley if she would sell a piece of land at a reduced rate to the California State Forestry Department to build a fire station. Mrs. Shipley, a Carlsbad resident since 1896, surprised her neighbors by giving the land outright for use as a State Forestry Station. Perhaps it was the example of Mrs. Shipley's philanthropy that prompted her daughter, Florence Shipley Magee, to donate her home to the city of Carlsbad almost forty years later. The land donated to the Forestry Station was located at the corner of Carlsbad Boulevard and Beech. It was directly across the street from the Shipley home. For the first time in the history of Carlsbad, there was a fire station located in town. State Forestry firemen under the direction of Chief Max Norwood constructed a sixty-nine-by-fifty-foot adobe firehouse as well as other buildings on the site during their spare time. Once World War II began in 1941, lack of manpower forced the State Forestry Service to call for volunteers to man the station. This action was helpful ten years later when Carlsbad decided to incorporate and founded its first volunteer fire department.

In 1939, another sign of prosperity occurred when ranunculi, narcissus, and anemone grower W. C. Garrett sold his entire bulb crop of twenty million flowers before the crop was even harvested. His fields, located south of Elm Avenue near Roosevelt, ran parallel to the train tracks and drew so much attention that the Santa Fe trains passing through town slowed down for the passengers' enjoyment. Special mention of Garrett and his willingness to walk visitors through the fields were touted in news articles, bringing people by the thousands to view the spring flowers. ❦

CHAPTER 6 The 1940s: World War II and the Hollywood Connection

World War II instigated many changes that affected Carlsbad during the war years and into the future, setting its course as an independent incorporated city. Carlsbad's population in 1941 hovered around 4,000, from which the city contributed over 220 men to military service.

World War II's impact hit Carlsbad immediately when Lee Ruse became the city's first war fatality, losing his life in the attack on Pearl Harbor. His church, the Carlsbad Community Church, dedicated a hall in his honor. Ruse was also remembered fondly by people in town. Maxton Brown, another war fatality, died flying over North Africa. He was remembered through the dedication of the Lieutenant Maxton Brown Bird Sanctuary overlooking Buena Vista Lagoon.

Royal Palms Motel, circa 1951. (Courtesy San Diego Historical Society)

In 1942, the U.S. Marine Corps moved to Rancho Santa Margarita and established Camp Pendleton. Arrival of the military in the area provided a wealth of opportunity for Carlsbad residents and helped turn the local economy around. Additionally, civilian workers were needed on base to fill a variety of jobs. Work on base provided income for Carlsbad residents, money that was spent in town bolstering the local economy. The need for civilian workers on base and for off-base housing and recreational facilities for military families all created new employment opportunities for Carlsbad residents.

The arrival of military personnel and their families at Camp Pendleton and Camp Elliott in La Jolla precipitated a housing shortage. So severe was the shortage that local newspapers ran editorials declaring that it was everyone's patriotic duty to rent space in their homes for the incoming military personnel and their families. Lack of sufficient housing prompted many military families to purchase homes. Additionally, local residents began buying vacant lots and constructing low-cost rental cottages. This influx of people caused a surge in Carlsbad real estate activity.

The Carlsbad Hotel contributed to the war effort by housing recuperating military personnel. Hollywood celebrities, such as Leo Carrillo, contributed to USO programs held next door at St. Michael's Hall. Carrillo visited with servicemen and brought guests who were staying at his Flying LC Ranch. With Hollywood stars attending the Carlsbad USO, it became an exciting venue and at the same time provided a safe and inviting environment for the GIs. Each church in town provided volunteer staff to welcome over 688 military personnel who attended each month.

Demolition of Royal Palms Chapel.

Many other locales within Carlsbad were commandeered by the military for use in the war effort. Private homes and businesses were transformed into military outposts throughout the

Demolition of Royal Palms.

city. The beach bluffs along Terramar became antiaircraft stations, the Cohn Estate on Carlsbad Boulevard was appropriated by the Coast Guard, a service station across from the Twin Inns on the same street was used as a Military Police Station, and Hosp Grove provided space needed by the U.S. Army to erect a tent city.

Fortunately for the Kentner family, the military rejected the Twin Inns use in the war effort, allowing the family to carry on with business as usual. Considering the war rationing under way, carrying on as usual for any business was a difficult proposition. However, Eddie Kentner, always resourceful and ingenious, found a way to work around the rationing issue by going into the poultry business himself and thus providing the needed supplies for his restaurant. By purchasing land on Sunnycreek Road outside of the downtown area of Carlsbad, Kentner was able to establish the Tootsie K Ranch in 1943. The Kentners built a small house with a reservoir and each family member had a turn at working on the ranch, raising the poultry needed to keep the Twin Inns in operation.

Hollywood made its presence felt in Carlsbad before, during, and after the war. Carlsbad's acquaintance with Hollywood was a long and varied one that dated as far back as 1923, when Mary Pickford and Douglas Fairbanks Sr. would camp along the banks of the Agua Hedionda Lagoon. As Prohibition overtook

Royal Palms, the former Cohn Estate.

America, Carlsbad was often a midway stopping off point for many folks traveling between Los Angeles and Tijuana, Mexico. Signed guest registers recorded the many Hollywood celebrities who stopped for dinner at the Twin Inns Restaurant. Baron Long, owner of Caliente Racetrack in Baja and Eddie Kentner's boss from his days at the Ships Cafe in Venice was a frequent visitor to the Twin Inns, as was Jack Dempsey, owner of the Casino in Ensenada, Mexico. When the California Carlsbad Hotel opened in the 1930s it provided another spot in Carlsbad for Hollywood celebrities, as well as other famous folks, to

relax. Men like Adolph Coors, the famous beer producer, the Bekins family of moving company fame, as well as professional baseball teams, all stayed in town. During the 1930s the Carlsbad Hotel was the site each year of the Bing Crosby special dinner dance that highlighted his annual Rancho Santa Fe Golf Tournament. The hotel provided rooms for over two hundred golfers, reporters, and onlookers who traveled to Rancho Santa Fe each day to attend the golfing event.

While many stars enjoyed the comforts offered at the Carlsbad Hotel while filming movies for the war effort at Camp Pendleton, other celebrities were simply interested in investing in Carlsbad real estate. Perhaps it was Bing Crosby's familiarity with Carlsbad that led him along with the Casey family and some other unnamed investors, to form a company called Carlsbad Properties in 1944. This company purchased the Cohn Estate on Carlsbad Boulevard and Elm Avenue, diagonal from the Twin Inns Restaurant. Plans were made to develop the property into the Royal Palms Motel and Sea Side Cafe. Opened at the end of World War II, the Royal Palms, with its swimming pool and wedding chapel, became a vacation destination, contributing to Carlsbad's post-war evolution from agricultural land to tourist spot.

CHAPTER 7

The Postwar Years and New Political Developments

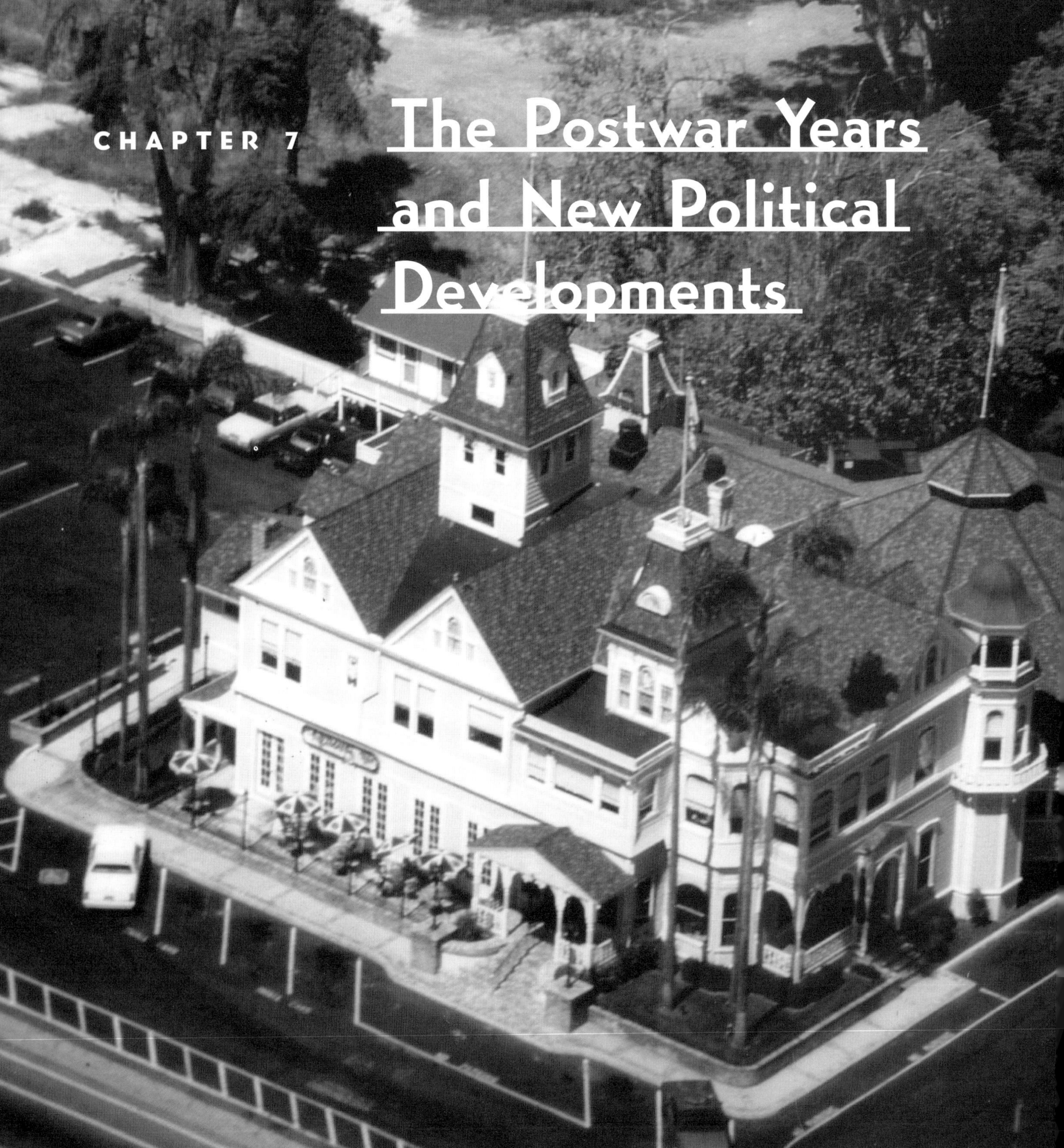

The many wartime changes that occurred in Carlsbad created a series of events that eventually had a major impact on Carlsbad's view of itself. By war's end, Carlsbad was thriving economically. The influx of military families had revived the real estate market and the business community. GIs settling in town created an environment that was different from the prewar years. The water system was overtaxed by the increase in population. Even construction of the Calaveras Dam was not a significant solution to the water problem. The postwar population increase placed a strain on the local school system causing overcrowding. The lack of basic services inadvertently set up a situation that eventually led to incorporation.

By the early 1950s a series of events led to a growing dissatisfaction with San Diego County's administration of Carlsbad. Residents believed that a better understanding of their problems and a faster solution to those problems would occur if civic matters were handled locally. Each problem or issue that Carlsbad faced was not enough of an individual reason to generate total support or a need for creating a new city. However, viewed together these issues functioned as building blocks to create a new Carlsbad identity. Some folks argued in favor of one particular "straw that broke the camel's back" that forced an incorporation vote. But the facts supported a series of independent events that joined at about the same time to create a unique window of opportunity that lead to formation of an independent city.

Twin Inns, 1987.

Twin Inns/Village Faire construction.

Carlsbad's first de facto government was the Chamber of Commerce, founded in 1923 by Roy Chase. Catering for many years to the fledgling business community, the Chamber worked in the best interest of all Carlsbad residents by focusing their combined efforts on finding solutions to local problems. Chamber members petitioned the San Diego County Supervisors for road improvements, building codes, street lighting, and updated sewer systems. It was the Chamber that paid for tourism advertisements and installation of street signs. The Chamber also began street beautification programs to clean up vacant land and plant trees and flowers throughout the downtown. As the city grew, so did the Chamber of Commerce workload. By the late 1940s the Chamber of Commerce had an organization of hard-working community-minded members with the expertise and reputation to handle a variety of civic business.

Dewey McClellan, son-in-law of Chamber founder Roy Chase and Chamber president himself in 1932 and 1946, was a well-respected man in Carlsbad. Viewed as honest, hardworking, and intelligent, many ordinary citizens sought his opinion and advice on community-related issues. According to Al Jandros, he and Reg Marron Sr. introduced Mr. Kay Kalika of Gorden Whitenall and Associates to Dewey McClellan. Kalika recommended to McClellan that Carlsbad might consider incorporation as a solution to the many problems facing the town. It was becoming increasingly obvious that the workload to just maintain the status quo in town was a tremendous burden on the Chamber of Commerce.

Jandros and Marron had hired Whitenall and Associates to evaluate property they owned that ran south of Buena Vista Creek. This property, which later became Plaza Camino Real Mall, had a high salt content from sea intrusion and was considered worthless for farming. The release in 1950 of the Standford Survey detailed projected population increases in San Diego County and the needed road additions and improvements to accommodate the increase. Jandros and Marron hoped that their worthless farmland could be good for commercial development. Kalika suggested that this land was a terrific site for commercial development since two roads that were slated for major improvements, Highway 78 and El Camino Real, surrounded it. However, Kalika pointed out to McClellan, Jandros, and Marron that developers for such a project preferred working with local governments, since they received quicker response on building issues than if they dealt with county bureaucracy.

Top: Village Faire/Twin Inns, 1990s.

Bottom: Afton Jandros is standing with her horse and an unidentified man at the current site of Plaza Camino Real Mall. Hosp Grove is in the background.

While this issue was taking shape on the northern end of town, another equally important and more immediate development was occurring along the ocean and Agua Hedionda Lagoon. In 1948, the San Diego Gas and Electric Company bought 110 acres along the Agua Hedionda Lagoon to construct a power plant. Development of the power plant would generate more than just electricity, it would produce a tremendous amount of tax money, funds that could be used to establish and maintain a city government. By the early 1950s the power plant represented a potential source of income to run a city. It was believed that incorporation and the formation of local government would solve many issues and problems. On

The Jandros family is standing at the corner of present-day Marron Road and El Camino Real.

January 1, 1952, an event that acted as a catalyst brought everything to a head.

A devastating house fire occurred on New Years Day 1952 which underlined Carlsbad's totally inadequate municipal services. By the time the fire was over, the series of events associated with it could only be termed a dark comedy of errors. Early on the morning of January 1, 1952, when smoke was first seen rising from the Garlock house, neighbors thought they were burning trash. Later in the day, at 2:40 p.m., people realized that the home was on fire and a call was placed to the State Forestry Station. The truck was out on another call but by 3:00 p.m. the truck arrived along with the Carlsbad Volunteer Fire Department crew. The problem was, they had no equipment to fight the fire. Finally at 3:15 p.m. Oceanside's Fire Department arrived and at 3:30 p.m. another State Forestry truck from Del Mar was on the scene, but there were no water hydrants close by. As a truck pumped out its tanks it had to go to Pine School on Harding Street to refill and then drive back to the Garlock home on Oak Street. By 6:00 p.m. the firefighters believed that the fire was under control and left. At 7:00 p.m. the fire rekindled, but the Carlsbad-based State Forestry Truck was in La Mesa. Del Mar, again sent their truck, which arrived at 8:00 p.m. and stayed until 11:00 p.m., when the fire was finally extinguished. Unfortunately, by this time, the Garlock home was totally destroyed.

The Battle for Incorporation

Carlsbad residents were incensed over their lack of locally controlled services. The fire just highlighted how precarious their position truly was concerning basic services. Letters of complaint started appearing in the local newspaper, outlining problems that faced the town. The list of concerns grew from the lack of basic fire and police service to a declining water supply, lack of fire hydrants, and an antiquated sewage system built in 1929. As the number of complaints rose, three separate factions evolved: Incorporationists, Annexationists, and Rural Citizens who supported maintaining the status quo. Each faction had a proposed solution for all the complaints. Incorporationists believed the only solution to the problems faced by Carlsbad residents was to take control of civic issues through formation of a city government. Annexationists believed that the easiest solution to their problems would be joining Oceanside, an existing city, and providing immediate access to all of their services. The Rural Citizens viewed all the hoopla as extremist. What had worked for years, relying on the San Diego County Supervisors to administer local business, was good enough and would not raise taxes.

Arguments for and against each viewpoint inundated the newspapers as editorials, news stories, and letters to the editor. So obvious was the *Carlsbad Journal*'s support of incorporation that the Rural Citizen faction started their own newspaper called the *Carlsbad Free Press*. It must be noted that while the three factions were divided on how best to solve Carlsbad's problems and issues, they were all united in the belief that something had to be done, some improvements had to be made for the good of the community.

In addition to the fire response time, another issue still unresolved that had been under discussion since 1949 was how to obtain water for Carlsbad. The Carlsbad Mutual Water Company (CMWC) was a stockholder-owned water company. It owned and operated water wells along the San Luis Rey River. The company piped water into Carlsbad. These wells kept increasing in salinity as well as drying up. CMWC was unable to finance construction of pipelines that would connect to the San Diego Water Authority aqueducts. The Public Utility District formed in 1949 to find a solution to the water issue, was also unable to solve the water problem. One of the reasons they were unsuccessful was they lacked any real power or authority. If a group refused to join the district, then there was no way to force them to comply. The San Diego Water Authority brought in water from the Colorado River. Carlsbad needed the water and had no way to raise the funds needed to connect to the San Diego Water Authority aqueducts. Without an adequate supply of water there would be no further residential or agricultural development in Carlsbad. An incorporated city would have the authority to finance construction of the pipelines needed to connect to the aqueducts.

For a United Independent Carlsbad

Vote FOR Carlsbad

For Member of the CITY COUNCIL — Vote for Five

MANUEL M. CASTORENA, Incumbent — X
RAYMOND C. EDE, Incumbent — X
C. D. McCLELLAN, Incumbent — X
LAWRENCE E. (LARRY) BUCHART, Industrial Engineer and Accountant
HERBERT L. CARPENTER, Builder
FRANK T. DOWNING, Retired
MANUEL M. GASTELUM
C. (RED) HELTON, Building Contractor — X
CLARK N. JOHNSTONE, Contracting Plumber
CHARLES B. LEDGERWOOD, Seedsman
FRANK B. SMITH, Retired
JANE C. SONNEMAN, Housewife — Businesswoman
ROBERT M. SUTTON — X
GORTON F. WHITE, Painter

For CITY CLERK — Vote for One

MAX O. EWALD — X
AFTON G. JANDRO, Houswife

For City Treasurer — Vote for One

W. ROY PACE, Incumbent — X

THESE CITIZENS (X) ARE MATURE, CAPABLE, EXPERIENCED LEADERS

They Are For An Independent CITY OF CARLSBAD

- WITH METROPOLITAN WATER IN THE MOST ECONOMICAL WAY
- CONTINUED LOW TAX RATES
- LOCAL GOVERNMENT BY LOCAL PEOPLE WITH PROGRESS IN A CONSERVATIVE, ORDERLY MANNER

VOTE TUESDAY, APRIL 13, 1954

United Carlsbad League

Sample election ballot from 1954.

After the New Year's Day fire in 1952, retired Major General W. W. Worton, a coastal strip resident, wrote a letter to the San Diego County Board of Supervisors, the Carlsbad Public Utilities Commission, and the *Carlsbad Journal*, which was printed on January 10, 1952. In this letter, Worton accused the County Board of Supervisors of not satisfying Carlsbad's needs by not considering how rapidly the town was growing and by not providing adequate fire and police service.

Colonel Gronseth of the Carlsbad Public Utilities Board answered General Worton's concerns. He clarified what specific areas the Carlsbad Public Utilities Board was authorized to address. It was Gronseth's opinion that better fire protection was possible, but establishment of a local police force or resolving health or sanitation issues were beyond the Public Utilities Commission's domain. Gronseth later suggested, when addressing the Carlsbad Chamber of Commerce, that incorporation could possibly offer a solution to the concerns and issues expressed by General Worton and by other Carlsbad residents.

Carlsbad Journal editor Robert Garland wrote articles that supported Colonel Gronseth's opinion regarding incorporation as the solution to Carlsbad's problems. He stated that the town was "growing without guidance and we must take steps to incorporate." The feasibility of incorporation now became an issue.

Looking west from Agua Hedionda Lagoon to Encina Power Plant, 2001.

INCORPORATION

Incorporation Election: June 24, 1952

Election Returns: 781-714

Election Returns after Absentee Ballots Are Counted: 809-732

Incorporation Inaugural Ceremonies: July 11, 1952

First Elected Carlsbad City Council: Dewey McClellan, George Grober, Ray Ede, Manuel Castorena, Lena Sutton

Would there be sufficient revenue to support a city if a successful incorporation election occurred? Committees were formed to study the issue, gathering information from neighboring cities and examining what it cost to run a city. Additionally, the committees needed to investigate the legal steps necessary for a successful election attempt. Studies were completed and the information was released in the January 31, 1952 edition of the *Carlsbad Journal*. San Diego County procedures for incorporation entailed three steps: a petition requesting an incorporation election signed by 25 percent of the affected property owners who owned at least 25 percent of the land; money deposited to defray the cost to publish the petition and notice of the election; and the boundaries set for the proposed incorporated city. After the petition was submitted to the San Diego County Board of Supervisors, a hearing would be set within two weeks, and an election within two months. Concurrent with an incorporation election, the first slate of city officials would be elected.

One of the basic steps to be determined was the actual size of the proposed City of Carlsbad. On February 19, 1952, the County Boundary Commission accepted the plan submitted by the Incorporationists, detailing the area that hopefully would be the future city of Carlsbad. The area was about seven square miles and included some of the original Rancho Agua Hedionda land grant as well as the downtown area developed by the Carlsbad Land and Water Company. The hoped for city would have a northern border that zigzagged through the Buena Vista Lagoon from the Pacific Ocean east to El Camino Real. The eastern boundary of the city would follow El Camino Real south to a point between the current Kelly Drive and Cannon Road. It would head west to the Agua Hedionda Lagoon and zigzag and drop south again to run parallel to the coast, about one mile inland from the ocean. It would finally join Palomar Airport Road, where it would turn west and continue until it reached the Pacific Ocean. The boundaries of the proposed City of Carlsbad were generally the same as those of the Carlsbad Utility District, except that the North Carlsbad (Fire Mountain) area would be left out. The reason Fire Mountain was excluded was simply the area was not contiguous to the rest of the proposed City of Carlsbad. The San Diego Gas and Electric Company's Encina Power Plant, while not included in the Public Utility District, was added to the proposed City Incorporation Boundaries Plan (*Carlsbad Journal*, February 21,1952).

During the Boundary Commission hearing, those in favor of annexation with Oceanside objected to their coastal property being included in the proposed City of Carlsbad boundaries. The Boundary Commission listened to all arguments presented by Oceanside City Attorney Harry Juliani, Paul Waggener, retired Major General Worton, and Colonel William Atkinson. They requested the Boundary Commission to leave the coastal strip out of the proposed City of Carlsbad. The Boundary Commission approved the boundaries as submitted by the Incorporationists and informed the Annexationists that they did so because of the Annexationists' failure to submit any boundary proposals of their own.

The reason that the Annexationists had failed to submit boundary proposals of their own was simply because they had not yet approached the Oceanside City Council with the request to be annexed. The Annexationists finally approached the Oceanside City Council on February 22, 1952, proposing that they annex only the land west of the railroad tracks in Carlsbad and from the Army and Navy Academy south to Pine Street.

Residents in that area of town who favored annexation believed it would provide an immediate solution for all their problems. Oceanside, which incorporated in 1898, was a well-established municipality with its own fire and police services, an ample supply of water, and adequate sanitation. Considering their own interests over the good of the entire town, many of the residents along the coastal strip started leaning towards annexation with Oceanside.

Oceanside agreed to accept the land in this proposed area into their city if an official petition was signed by at least 25 percent of the property owners and a majority subsequently voted in favor of annexation. On February 23, 1952, an

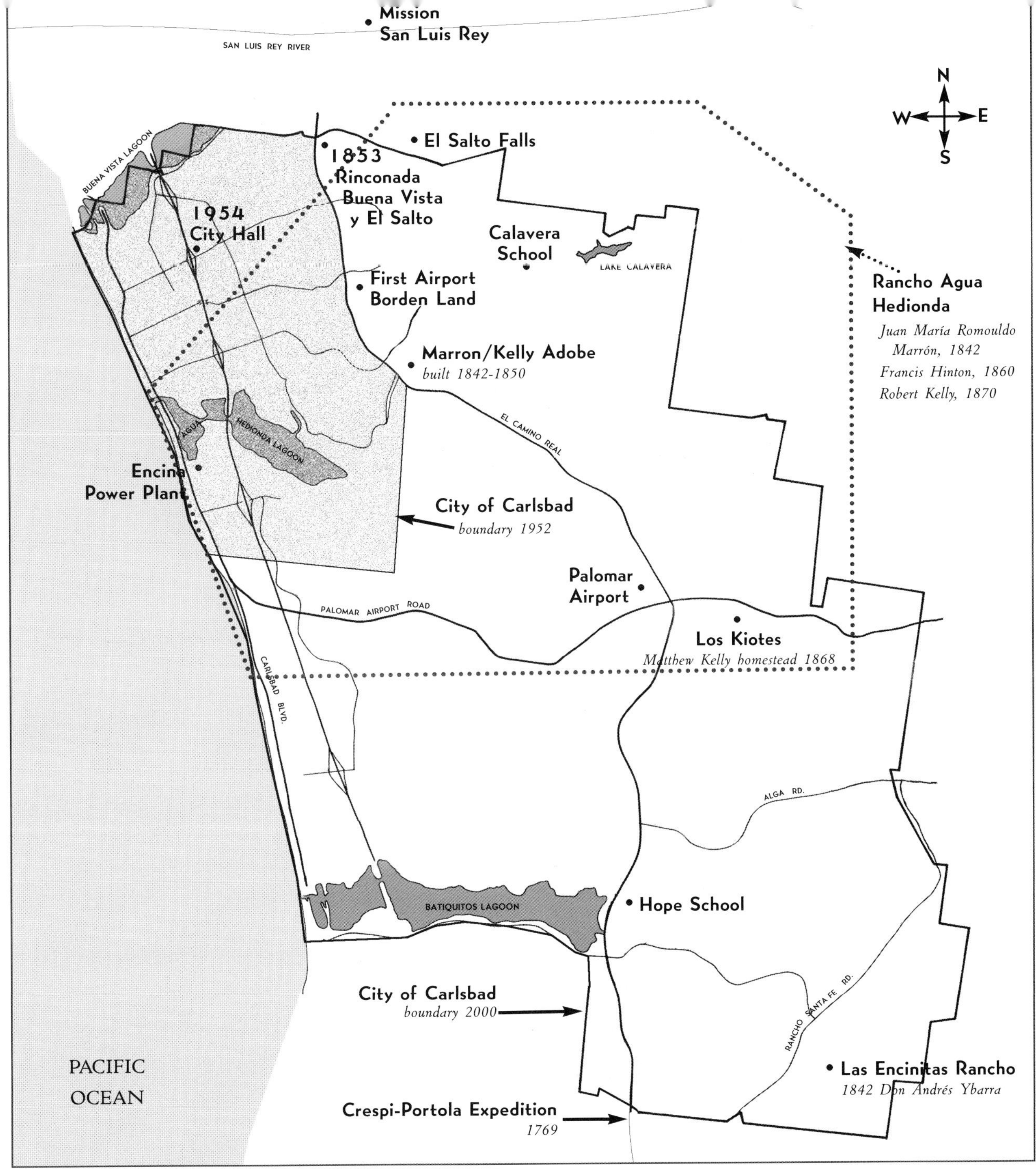

Boundary map of present-day Carlsbad, initial incorporated city, land grants, Agua Hedionda (dotted line), and Las Encinitas Rancho (bottom right).

Annexation Committee was formed and an official annexation petition was started. Three days later, on February 26, 1952, Attorney J. R. Goodbody submitted eighteen petitions with several hundred signatures requesting an incorporation election. The San Diego County Board of Supervisors accepted them unanimously at their meeting, pending signature verification. Before this meeting was terminated, Oceanside City Attorney Juliani claimed that Oceanside had "preempted" the coastal area that was included in the proposed City of Carlsbad by agreeing to accept petitions from residents in that area for annexation.

Carlsbad Boulevard looking south towards Encina power plant, 1988.

Juliani also stated that Oceanside had the right to decide if they were annexing the land or not before it could be included in the proposed City of Carlsbad. San Diego County Counsel Bertram McLees disagreed, stating that Oceanside had no legal jurisdiction over the Carlsbad coastal land. There had been no legal petitions filed for annexation and Oceanside had just agreed four days before to accept any circulated and signed petitions from this group of residents.

On March 4, 1952, one and a half hours after Marie Nasland, clerk to the San Diego County Board of Supervisors, certified that the incorporation petitions were in order, more than $2,000 was deposited to cover legal and advertising expenses for the incorporation election.

On March 10, 1952, the official annexation petition was submitted to and accepted by the Oceanside City Council. This petition had signatures from fifty-seven of the ninety coastal strip registered voters. At their March 10 meeting, the Oceanside City Council invited Carlsbad residents living west of the proposed future I-5 freeway and all the way south to Batiquitos Lagoon to join the annexation to Oceanside. Their offer was extended to those areas of Carlsbad that offered some financial value to Oceanside, not to the more rural areas that needed the protection of city services just as much if not more than the downtown areas.

Residents of the noncoastal areas of Carlsbad that could have accepted the Oceanside offer were not interested in annexation with Oceanside. These residents ran a real risk by holding out for incorporation, since the entire issue would be moot if the coastal area annexed to Oceanside. The coastal area contained some of the most lucrative tax producers in Carlsbad: the Army and Navy Academy, the Carlsbad Hotel, the Royal Palms Motel, and the San Diego Gas and Electric Power Plant. If the coastal area joined Oceanside there would be no way the rest of Carlsbad could financially afford to incorporate. Lack of funds from the coastal strip would mean not enough money to lay new sewer or water lines to join with the Metropolitan Water District and it would eliminate the tax money needed to improve increasingly overcrowded schools. It became obvious that annexation of Carlsbad's coastal strip would eliminate the need for incorporation, since there would not be sufficient tax funds to pay for city services.

Despite the concerns of all the other Carlsbad residents, the Annexationists forged on with their plans, setting May 2, 1952, as the date for election. While the Annexationists were busy with their plans, the Incorporationists continued working towards their goal of one unified city. Incorporation Committee Chair Colonel Gronseth held informational meetings at the Carlsbad School auditorium throughout March of 1952. Incorporation Committee Attorney J. R. Goodbody, School Superintendent Walter Glines, Sanitary District Representative Edger Charles Anthony, and Eddie Kentner all advocated for incorporation and gave factual information to interested attendees.

During April the County Board of Supervisors held several public hearings on the proposed incorporation boundaries, and members of all three factions attended. Each group presented their case, reiterating their previous arguments and adding a few new ones, such as how loss of the beach would affect Carlsbad residents if the coastal strip annexed to Oceanside. Attendees questioned who protected coastal strip residents who did not want to annex to Oceanside. Claude Fennel, a pro-Incorporationist stated, "It was not fair, to let half a dozen people [those in favor of annexation] decide Carlsbad's future" (*Carlsbad Journal*, April, 10, 1952). It was a valid point, considering that removal of the coastal strip would limit any hope of economic viability for Carlsbad.

Three days before the May 2 annexation vote, the County Board of Supervisors finally approved the proposed city of Carlsbad boundaries as submitted by the Incorporationist faction on February 19. These boundaries included the Carlsbad coastal strip and the SDG&E Encina power plant then under construction.

On May 2, 1952, the annexation vote proceeded at 7:00 a.m. in the lobby of the Carlsbad Hotel. With election results in doubt, (forty-four votes in favor to forty-one opposed, five absentee ballots and five disputed ballots waiting to be counted), the county set the incorporation election date for June 24, 1952.

Annexation election results were revealed on May 14 when absentee ballots were opened and counted at the scheduled

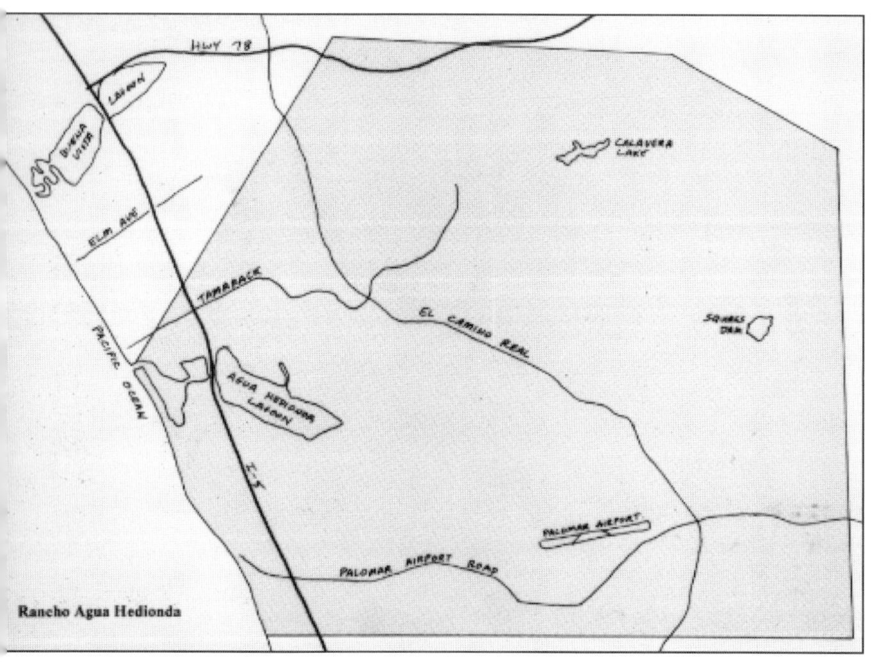

Rancho Agua Hedionda.

Oceanside City Council meeting. Banner headlines "Strip Annexation Loses" blazed across the May 15 edition of the *Carlsbad Journal.* A tie vote of forty-five to forty-five defeated the annexation attempt, since a simple majority was needed. Those who worked diligently for annexation then turned their attention to supporting incorporation as the only viable solution to Carlsbad's many issues of adequate sanitation, water, fire, and police service.

During the next six weeks, the Incorporationists continued with their informational meetings at the Carlsbad School. They organized committees, nominated future council members, and appointed precinct workers. At this point, with the annexation issue resolved, the Incorporationists faced vocal accusations from the rural citizens, who wished to maintain the status quo and stay unincorporated and dependent on the San Diego County Board of Supervisors.

The Rural Citizens Group was made up of farmers, gardeners, and orchardists, for the most part successful agriculturalists. This group objected to incorporation because they believed it would adversely affect their farming business by increasing taxes, eventually forcing them to sell their land. They viewed those in favor of incorporation as progressives who wished to eliminate farmers in order to build subdivisions and increase development. The plan that the Rural Citizens presented to the rest of Carlsbad's voting population was rather confusing. They proposed presenting a slate of five candidates for City Council if the incorporation vote passed. If this slate of candidates was elected, they would then dissolve the incorporation and annex to Oceanside. This argument seemed illogical and failed to win a majority of the voters. Their own argument that belonging to a city was bad for farming seemed to be self-defeating.

Carlsbad Journal editorials answered a variety of points raised each week by the Rural Citizens Group. However, a few remarks made by members of this group bordered on slanderous accusations, implying that personal gain by the business community was the underlying reason for incorporation. At this point the *Carlsbad Journal* moved their editorial comments from the inside pages of the newspaper to the front page. They began to name those Rural Citizens who were making these accusations. The Rural Citizens were accused of making false accusations and of running an eleventh-hour smear campaign to save a few pennies in tax money.

On June 24, 1952, the election for incorporation took place. Incorporation won 781 to 714. The first City Council chosen in this election included: Manuel Castorena, Raymond Ede, George Grober, C. D. McClellan, and Lena Sutton with Roy Pace as treasurer.

A public service booklet published at the time by the Union Title Insurance and Trust Company stated, "On June 24, 1952, in a special election, residents of Carlsbad voted to incorporate. The splendid cooperation between various service organizations in Carlsbad plus the undeniable natural advantages of the community itself, combine to help paint a rosy picture of Carlsbad's future." This was a prophecy that seems to have come true.

View of original city boundary, looking west from Hosp Grove.

CHAPTER 8 Early Government

The First Employees and New Infrastructure

"It takes work to establish a city." Editor Buzz Garland expressed this sentiment in the *Carlsbad Journal.* Once Carlsbad's certificate of incorporation was filed on July 16, 1952, the City Council held their first meeting. At this meeting, Council members divided up the workload facing the city. Each member agreed to chair one of the citizen volunteer committees that were formed to gather information pertaining to water, police, fire, building, public works, finance, budget, zoning, and planning.

The newly elected City Council began forming a city government by assuming all government responsibilities and duties previously handled by the San Diego County Board of Supervisors. The Council also initiated a local control of government in Carlsbad. They issued a statement promising to proceed slowly and thoughtfully while setting the basic city infrastructure in place. Operating funds were limited and the Council depended on volunteer labor and expertise. Carlsbad's initial city budget was derived solely from permits and business license fees. Collecting funds from gas taxes, liquor licenses, and motor vehicle fees was several months away and property tax fees would not be available for at least eighteen months.

Terramar subdivision, circa 1957. (Courtesy San Diego Historical Society)

Ede Westree.

Since the budget was limited, the Council could hire employees only as they were absolutely needed or as funds became available. The City of Carlsbad's first employee was Attorney T. Bruce Smith. He was hired for a sixty-day trial period at $300 a month to draw up city ordinances and to do preliminary legal work. Some of the legal concerns facing the Council were lawsuits filed by Clifton and Alma Williams and C. H. Patterson that questioned the validity of Carlsbad's incorporation. The city attorney's salary was well spent when he successfully defended Carlsbad's right to incorporate.

According to Ede Westree, Colonel Edward Hagen, Carlsbad's first elected city clerk, refused to take even one cent in salary. The retired U.S. Army colonel believed in serving the community. Colonel Hagen received permission from the Carlsbad branch of the State Forestry Department for temporary use of their building on Beech and Carlsbad Boulevard for city office space. He established nine-to-five office hours and hired Virginia Amburgey in September as a clerk-typist. Mrs. Natalie Vermilyea replaced Ms. Amburgey, who resigned in December 1952. Mrs. Vermilyea had already contributed many volunteer hours working for the city and made a smooth transition into her new job. Mrs. Vermilyea was well known as a jack-of-all-trades when she became Carlsbad's first policewoman.

By the end of 1952, Carlsbad had converted itself from a small town into a fledgling city. It was San Diego County's ninth city to incorporate and the first to do so in forty years. The city consisted of 7.5 square miles with a population of 6,963. As a general law city, it followed the laws of the state of California rather than a specific city charter. The nascent city had no budget, buildings, land, or public works department. The five city employees, City Clerk Colonel Ed Hagen, City Treasurer Roy Pace, City Attorney T. Bruce Smith, Police Chief Max Palkowski, and Clerk-Secretary Natalie Vermilyea worked diligently for the residents of Carlsbad.

South from Buena Vista Lagoon, circa 1960s.

Throughout the 1950s, Carlsbad established all basic city services, increased the budget to $401,028 and employed forty-two full-time staff. In 1952 the Carlsbad Police Department was formed and Max Palkowski was hired as police chief. Max Ewald was hired in 1953 as the city's first building inspector. By 1954, the city budget, supplemented by S.D.G.&E. taxes, increased enough to hire Floyd Hollowell as the first full-time fireman, Nelson Westree as parks superintendent, Jack Kubota as city engineer, and Ralph Scholink as director of finance and also to establish the Carlsbad Municipal Water District.

The office of city manager was established in 1955 when the Council passed an ordinance creating the position in response to the increased workload. Herbert Nelson, a retired U.S. Marine who was hired as city manager at a salary of $500 a month, assumed the daily management of the city. Carlsbad's first city library was established in 1956. Georgina Cole, Carlsbad's county branch librarian, persuaded the City Council to remove Carlsbad from the San Diego County library system and create a city library system.

A series of events affected Carlsbad during the 1950s, including construction of I-5, and of San Diego Gas and Electric's Encina power plant, acquisition of Colorado River water, and a continued legal struggle with the Rural Citizens Group.

In November 1953, the first 10.7 miles of Interstate 5 connecting Carlsbad to Oceanside was dedicated. The freeway bisected the city and diverted traffic from the Coast Highway, drawing customers away from the downtown business district. It also made travel within Carlsbad from one side of the freeway to the other more difficult. The only roads that connected east to west through Carlsbad were Tamarack and Elm. The Chestnut underpass was not available and neither were the bridges over

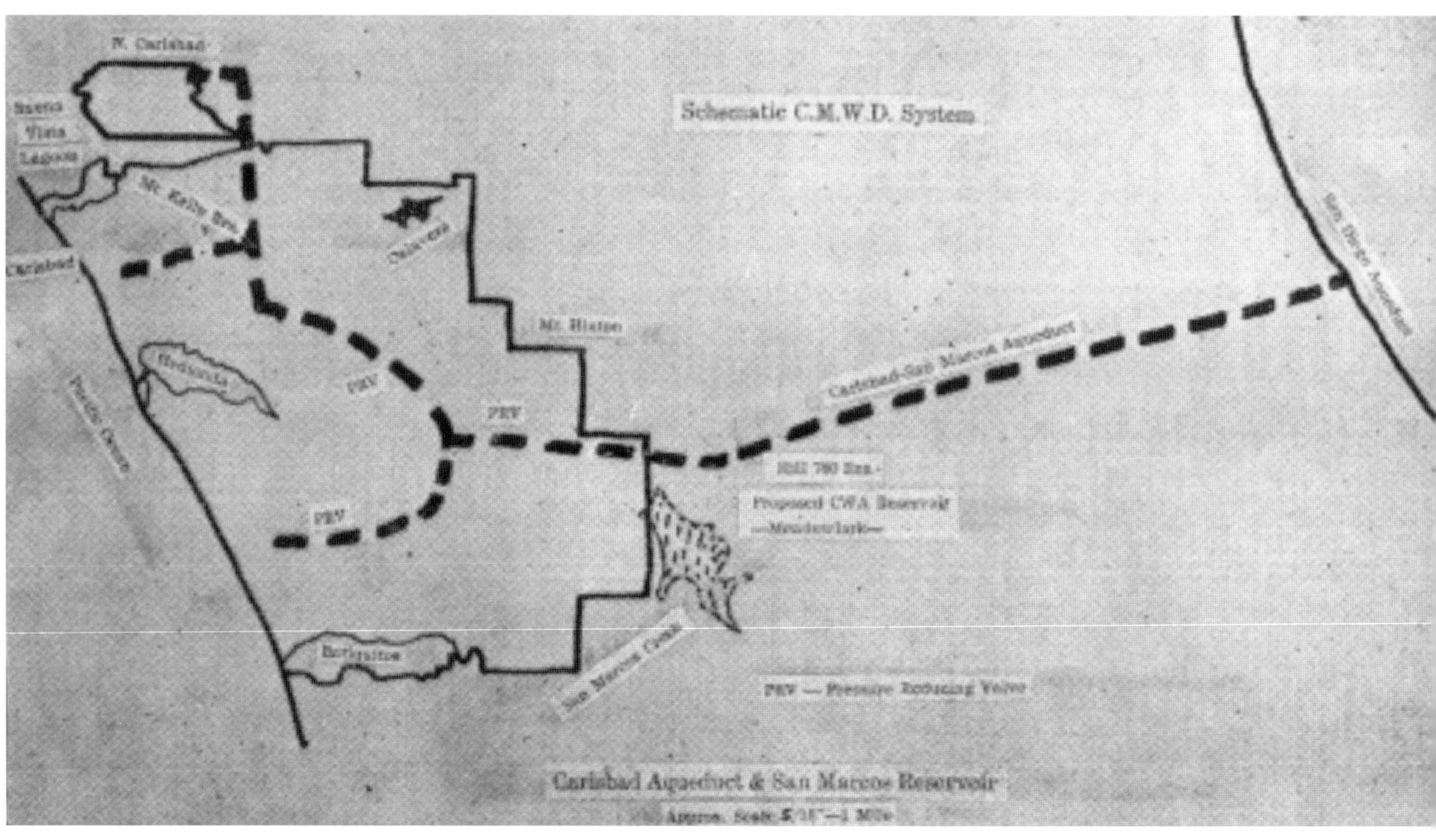

Drawing of proposed Carlsbad Municipal Water district pipeline printed in 1955 Carlsbad Journal.

Chinquapin and Jefferson. Many farms that once grew beans, strawberries, and flowers were paved over when the freeway went directly through their fields. The only benefit the freeway offered to Carlsbad at this time was faster travel to Oceanside. The City Council was faced with the problem of increased traffic into town and the need for stoplights, signs, and general traffic control. Funds were requested from the state to help rectify some of the impacts caused by the freeway's construction.

In January 1952, San Diego Gas and Electric broke ground for their Encina power plant. Constructed on the southern bank of the Agua Hedionda Lagoon, the power plant provided local employment opportunities and a substantial amount of tax money. The existence of the power plant provided a secure source of revenue for the City of Carlsbad's budget. It was a fortuitous occurrence for Carlsbad that the natural resources of ocean and lagoon could provide the perfect environment for a power plant location. The ocean allowed easy and convenient unloading of fuel needed to operate the plant and the lagoon supplied an ample supply of water to cool the generating units. In 1954 the first generating unit of the Encina power plant was completed and functional. During the next two decades the plant expanded with the addition of four more generating units and with construction of a higher smokestack.

Finding and Developing Sources of Water

One of the biggest concerns during the 1950s was acquisition of water. Lack of water was one of the driving forces behind incorporation. Availability of water had always been an issue for Carlsbad residents. Having a water supply meant growth and development for the city.

Some families drew water from their own wells; others bought or were issued stock in the shareholder-owned Carlsbad Mutual Water Company. The Mutual pumped water from six wells along the San Luis Rey River. Carlsbad's water supply diminished during the 1940s for a variety of reasons. The salinity level rose in the wells as the wells along the San Luis Rey River started to go dry. A drought also contributed to the decrease in available water. Another factor was the increase in postwar population. As more people drew on the water supply, there was less water available.

The Carlsbad Mutual Water Company in 1953 supplied about one-third of their total water output to the newly incorporated city. The other two-thirds of the water went for agricultural use outside of the incorporated city. This water was of agricultural quality. The San Diego Board of Health repeatedly warned the Carlsbad Mutual Water Company to improve the water used domestically. Lack of adequate storage and filtration allowed foreign matter into the water supply. Consumers complained about taste and about rust particles in the water due to faulty pipelines and water mains. Those who lived in the downtown area and who could not afford to buy stock in the Carlsbad Mutual Water Company sank their own wells. The water was easy to access because the level was very close to the surface. However, there was not a sufficient difference in depths between water wells and septic systems and seepage between the two occurred. The County Health Department investigated contamination between the water systems and the septic systems when an outbreak of illnesses occurred in the Mexican neighborhood during 1952.

Carlsbad residents wanted a dependable and clean water supply. The San Diego Water District had a dependable and clean supply of Colorado River water. Carlsbad residents could obtain the water if pipelines from Carlsbad connected to the aqueduct. The cost to join the San Diego County Water District was $57,000 paid over a five-year period. The Carlsbad Mutual did not have the money to join the water district or lay new pipeline.

A second water company was established in March 1954 when Carlsbad residents overwhelmingly voted 1,189 to 644 to form the Carlsbad Municipal Water District. This district, known as CMWD, would cover over thirty thousand acres and was authorized to connect with the San Diego County Water district and obtain Colorado River water. Four directors were elected to the CMWD: W. W. Rogers, Max Ewald, Billy Fry, and Allan Kelly. CMWD used an Oceanside water line to bring water into Carlsbad, until a more permanent arrangement was made. A series of bond elections were held to finance the construction of pipeline. In August 1955 and July 1956, these bonds were defeated. Finally, in October 1956, a bond passed 1,500 to 577, financing the pipeline needed to connect with the aqueduct. The CMWD estimated the cost of running these pipelines would be to $6 a year per tax bill for thirty years.

The deterioration in water supply and equipment forced the Carlsbad Mutual to seek outside funding. The division of stock ownership in the privately owned Mutual Water Company, made it difficult to reach a voting quorum or a consensus of opinion from the shareholders. This made the Carlsbad Mutual Water

CITY SEAL

City Seal designed by Major Albert F. Rinehart in 1958.

In November 1958, the Carlsbad City Council announced a contest to design a City Seal, with a prize of $25 to the winner. Retired Major Albert F. Rinehart, who lived in town, saw the announcement while recovering from surgery and decided to enter the contest. Major Rinehart made a few rough sketches and submitted six different designs. The Council considered four of Rinehart's entries. The Rinehart design chosen by the City Council as the winner incorporated several symbolic representations of Carlsbad themes. The seal has an oval within which is centered a triad that represents Carlsbad's mayor-manager-council form of government. Superimposed on the triad is a symbol of a democratic government, which looks similar to a hatchet. There are three remaining segments, each of which represents Carlsbad's geography. On top of the triad are a sun and a sea, representing the climate and the coastal location of the city. Located on the bottom left of the triad is the official city flower, the bird of paradise or strelitzia reginae. This flower was developed for commercial use by local Carlsbad grower Clint Pedley and adopted as the city flower in 1952. On the bottom right of the triad is a cornucopia signifying Carlsbad's horticultural abundance.

The mosaic copy of the City Seal was made by John McKaig and hung in City Council chambers in 1979.

State Street looking north, circa late 1960s/early 1970s.

Company difficult to administer.

In August 1957 the Carlsbad Mutual Water Company Board of Directors unanimously voted to sell all Mutual Company assets to the city of Carlsbad. They stated four reasons for the sale: 1) Change in water use from rural to urban; 2) Subdivision of land that led to division of shares, resulting in higher administration costs; 3) Greater burden to administer divided shares; and 4) Sale would give the city control and ownership of a water distribution system that served a large percentage of city's population.

The city agreed to buy the Carlsbad Mutual Water Company if two conditions were met. The first was that shareholders had to agree to the sale and second that city voters needed to approve the sale contract and issuance of bonds to buy the Mutual's assets.

The city believed purchase of the Mutual would benefit the citizens of Carlsbad. It would save money for water users by elimination of duplication of services and equipment. Ownership of the Mutual would further reduce the fire insurance premiums and provide a more reliable source of water for those currently outside the CMWD. The city agreed to maintain and protect the water rights of the current Mutual customers. They also agreed to two different rate structures for water purchase. Agricultural water use would be charged a lower rate than that of domestic water use. The city also agreed to charge no more than an additional five cents in water rates for those Carlsbad Mutual customers that lived outside of the city limits. The city incurred all Mutual Company indebtedness and assumed all contracts. Finally, the city agreed to hire all Mutual employees for one year.

In December 1957, two bond issues were voted on. One bond issue authorized the purchase of the Carlsbad Mutual Water Company and the other authorized rehabilitating the existing equipment. Both bond issues passed by a strong majority. The Terramar Water System was added into the City Water

System in February 1958. By July of the same year, Carlsbad pipelines were directly connected with the aqueduct supplying Colorado River water. Once all areas of Carlsbad had a sufficient supply of potable water, the land value increased.

Incorporation Challenged

The Rural Citizen Group's opposition to incorporation in 1952 continued after the city was established. They had feared that new city services would cause new forms of taxation, which would eventually force them out of Carlsbad. City Attorney T. Bruce Smith successfully defended several lawsuits filed against the city by members of the Rural Citizens opposition. The first lawsuit filed within days of the election by Clifton and Alma Williams claimed that taxpayers would suffer if incorporation went through. They additionally charged that the *Carlsbad Journal*'s advocacy of incorporation had caused biased public support that influenced the voters. A second lawsuit was filed by C. H. Patterson in 1954. He contended that the incorporation was invalid because election notification was not given with two weeks advance notice and that the exact date had not been published in the *Carlsbad Journal*. The Fourth District Court of Appeals ruled in favor of Carlsbad's incorporation. The last challenge by the Rural Citizen's Group was made in March 1954. Forty-six Carlsbad residents requested Oceanside to annex Carlsbad. The Oceanside City Council agreed if they could get 25 percent of Carlsbad registered voters to sign a petition requesting a special annexation election. Carlsbad Mayor Dewey McClellan and the City Council protested Oceanside's actions. McClellan stated, "This action was prompted by persons within the city who were determined to halt the city's growth and who were unwilling to accept the verdict of the election." This was the last effort by any member of the Rural Citizen Group to reverse the results of the 1952 incorporation election. Mayor McClellan made overtures to several of the more rational members of this group, who later joined city government.

As Buzz Garland said in 1952, "It takes work to build a city." All the issues that led to incorporation were solved within six years of the election. The city had locally controlled Police and Fire Departments, adequate water, and a government that was concerned only with making Carlsbad a better place to live.

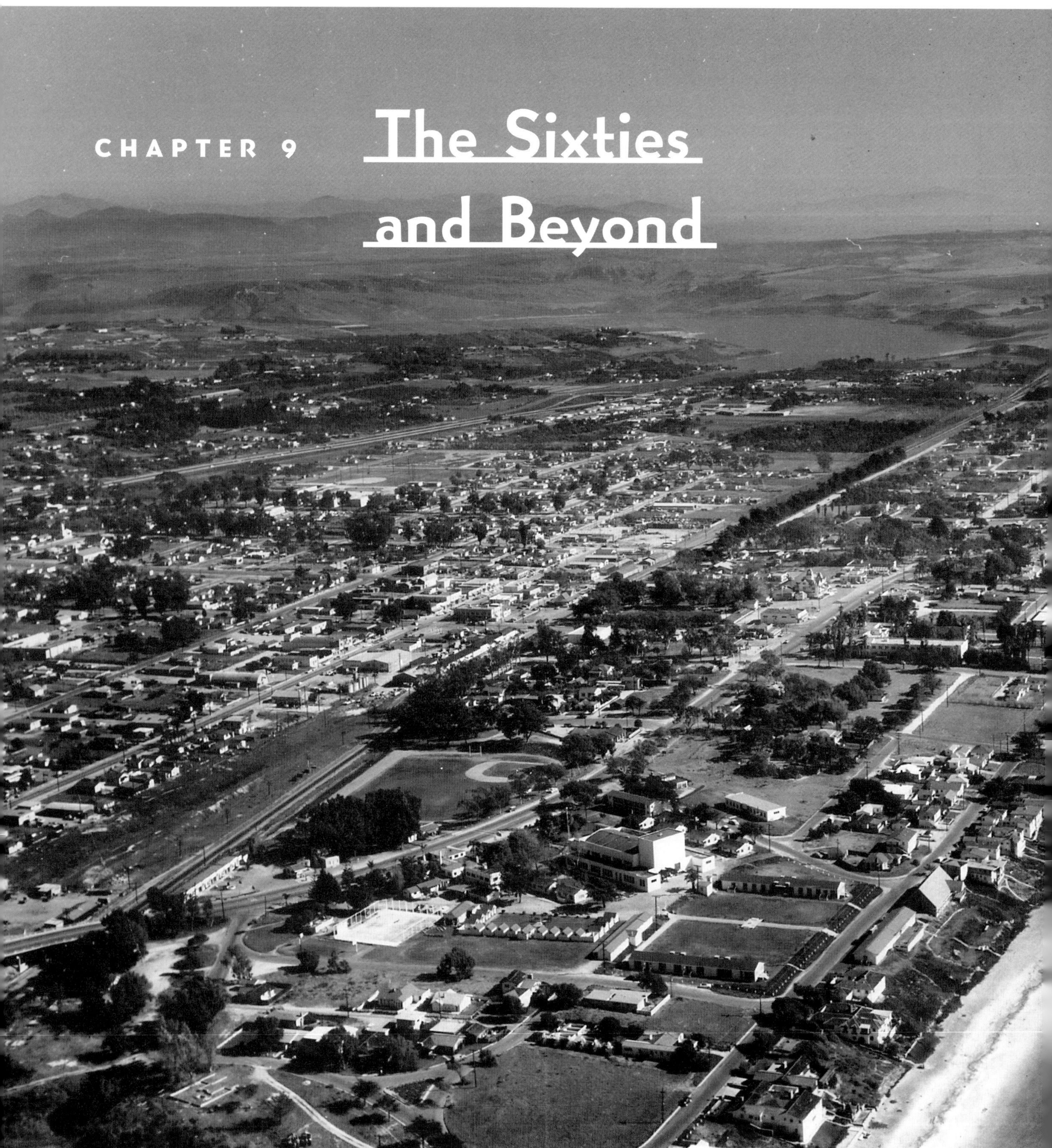

CHAPTER 9

The Sixties and Beyond

The Landscape Changes

The sixties was a decade when Carlsbad planned for the future. No longer concerned with only organizing the basic services that a city must have, city government could focus attention on constructing civic buildings and programs. The city worked towards finding ways to increase sources of tax revenue. The construction of light industry and residential and commercial development added tax money to the city budget. This in turn helped to finance new city programs. As the city began a series of land annexations, Carlsbad's geographical borders expanded, thus increasing the size and economic viability of the city. Planning for the future, Carlsbad defined a series of goals, which included finding ways to improve existing problems, formulating a general plan for future growth, constructing adequate civic buildings to service the growing community, and establishing a secure financial tax base.

Downtown Carlsbad looking south from Buena Vista Lagoon, circa 1957.

The first building constructed by the City of Carlsbad in 1954 was located on Pio Pico Drive and Elm Avenue. It housed Carlsbad City Hall, and the Police and Fire Department offices. (Byrd Collection)

One goal that the City Council set was finding solutions to preexisting problems in the downtown area. In 1961, complaints arose regarding the lack of street lighting, rezoning of certain areas, lack of adequate sewage disposal, decrepit housing, and no freeway underpass at Chestnut. The downtown area was desperately in need of improvement. Construction of Interstate 5 had divided the city in half. The lack of roads connecting the downtown section of Carlsbad to the areas east of the freeway made it difficult for students to get to the newly constructed high school. The Santa Fe Railroad, which ended passenger and freight service to Carlsbad by 1960, left its station depot as an abandoned eyesore in the downtown district. Many streets needed repaving, adequate sewage to stop the seasonal street flooding, and improved street lighting.

In one downtown section, some of the housing was unfit for human habitation. Many of the units used for housing in the downtown area that were declared unfit for human habitation by Dick Osburn, Carlsbad's Building Commissioner, were converted garages. Used as rental units, these buildings lacked proper sanitation, had defective wiring, too many people living in them, and only six-foot-high ceilings. Osburn declared these units would need at least a 50 percent remodel to make them safe for human habitation. Gradual rehabilitation of these units occurred when seventeen of them were demolished and were replaced with housing that conformed to city building codes.

In July 1961, the Planning Commission granted a zoning change for one section of Roosevelt Street at the request of Baltazar Aranda. The area known as the "Roosevelt Zone," included Tyler, Roosevelt, Madison, Walnut, and Oak was changed from R-P (residential-professional) to C-2 (general commercial) zoning. This increased the commercial tax revenues for the city and allowed for an expansion of the business community in town.

Agua Hedionda Lagoon in spring.

As the sixties progressed, the City Council continued with downtown improvements: streets were paved; drainage was installed that eliminated the ponds that formed along Grand Avenue after each rain; and the Elm Avenue lighting project was accomplished. During Mayor David Dunne's administration, funds were obtained that financed the $1-million Chestnut Street underpass construction, which was completed in 1971. This underpass greatly facilitated travel in town. It was particularly helpful as a direct route for all schoolchildren who lived west of the freeway and attended school east of the freeway.

Chris Christiansen, who was instrumental in obtaining the Old Santa Fe Depot for city use, convinced the members of Carlsbad's Rotary Club to donate time and funds to rehabilitate the building. The Rotary Club was successful in converting an eyesore into a small downtown park.

Sewage Solutions

Carlsbad and Vista agreed in 1961 that in order for their cities to grow, they needed to improve the existing sewage system. In order to accomplish this, they recognized the necessity of entering into a joint powers agreement specifically to solve this issue.

Agua Hedionda Lagoon in spring.

The plan they devised called for construction of an entirely new treatment plant built at Encina that connected to a mile-long concrete ocean outfall pipe. The Encina plant would replace the sewage treatment facility built in 1929 on Buena Vista Lagoon, near Highways 101 and 78. Taxpayers approved the sewage treatment plant bonds in 1962. The approval of a $2.12-million bond in Carlsbad and a $2,750,000 bond in Vista financed the construction of the Encina plant. Financial arrangements were later made to admit Buena Sanitation District and San Marcos City Water District into the Encina Sewage Treatment Facility. By the fall of 1965 the plant was built and operational.

Master Planning

Another city goal was to formulate a General or Master Plan that would map the city's future growth and give clear directions on how the city would obtain goals set in the plan. The city had adopted a county land use plan and a set of zoning codes immediately after incorporating in 1952. They operated under these guidelines until the 1960s, when substandard housing in the downtown area, and increased commercial, industrial, and residential growth as well as increased traffic and the annexation of more land brought on the need for planned growth. By December 1965, the City Council approved the Planning Department's preliminary General Plan, pending public input. Consisting of forty-one pages, the first General Plan, adopted in 1966, charted Carlsbad's growth for the next twenty years. The Plan was to be reviewed every year and revised every five years, adapting to changes in civic and community requirements. Elements of Carlsbad's General Plan had to interact with each other as well as with plans and programs at national, state, regional, and local levels.

Some of the elements contained in Carlsbad's General Plan were added in the years following the initial plan adoption. The Housing element, added in 1969, was the first added amendment to the approved General Plan. Today, after much revision, the Carlsbad General Plan covers land use, circulation (traffic), noise, housing, open space and conservation, public safety, parks and recreation, and arts. Hundreds of pages long, the Plan reflects Carlsbad's expanded city borders and the complex issues facing the city.

Aerial view of new City Hall, Library, and Fire Station after realignment of Pio Pico and widening of Interstate 5, circa 1969.

New Civic Facilities and Expansions

The physical growth of Carlsbad was another goal set during the sixties. The city built three large publicly owned buildings: City Hall, Fire Station No. 1, and the Library. Annexation of land that increased city boundaries and added more taxable land into the city also began during this decade. The construction of new industry, housing subdivisions, and commercial outlets also contributed to the physical and financial growth of the city.

In the late sixties, construction began on a series of civic buildings. More than thirty years after construction, these buildings are still in use. By the mid-sixties, Carlsbad citizens had outgrown their small library located in the old water department. Children and adult services were divided between two separate buildings. The need for a larger city library was obvious. The voters approved a bond issue that financed the construction of the new facility built on Elm Avenue that opened in 1967. This building is still used as a library and is currently known as the Georgina Cole Library. It became a focal point for community cultural experiences, providing thousands of volumes of books, art displays, lectures, film series, and community events.

State Street business district, circa 1960. (Courtesy San Diego Historical Society)

The first building that was constructed with city funds specifically for city office space was located on Elm and Pio Pico in 1954. It housed City Hall offices, the Police Department, and the Fire Department. In 1968 this building was demolished when Interstate 5 was widened. The city was forced at that time to rebuild their city complex. On September 8, 1968, the newly constructed City Hall and Police Department complex was dedicated. These buildings were located on a site, fronting the realigned Pio Pico and Elm location. The Fire Department was relocated into a separate building located diagonally from City Hall on Elm Street.

A series of land annexations during the sixties increased Carlsbad's area from 7.5 square miles to 11.3 square miles. The 1952 Incorporation boundaries marked Carlsbad's easternmost border as El Camino Real and set the southern border just south of the Agua Hedionda Lagoon. Annexation of various strips of land surrounding the city established new northern, eastern, and southern borders. One strip, annexed in 1963, ran east from Palomar Airport for two miles and incorporated the future Carlsbad Raceway. The industrial, commercial, and residential growth potential resulting from these land annexations provided

Carlsbad with a secure financial future.

Residential development that boomed during the sixties also contributed to Carlsbad's tax revenues. One of the largest developers, Kamar Construction Company, organized and run by Robert and Jerry Rombotis, built numerous subdivisions in Carlsbad such as Falcon Hills, Tamarack Manor, and Holiday Manor. In 1969, the old Carlsbad Airport near Chestnut and El Camino was converted into a subdivision of one hundred homes called El Camino Mesa. The La Costa Resort and surrounding homes were built in the mid-sixties. While technically not part of Carlsbad until 1972, the development of this area and the increase in population had a major impact on the city.

Undeveloped land annexed into city.

Impacts on Agriculture and New Revenue Sources

Residential and industrial development that replaced agricultural land in the city led to citizen complaints. Carlsbad's mayor, David Dunne, responded to these charges in April 1969. Dunne stated, "A lot of people here are not too anxious to see the city grow, but you can't put a fence around it. People are going to

Plaza Camino Real Mall, circa 1970s.

Right, below: El Salto Falls off of Haymar Road, northeast Carlsbad site of South Coast Asphalt Company Rock quarry. (Caron Collection)

come and we have to take care of them. We've had pretty much an agricultural/tourist type economy, but we have to develop our industrial base to keep taxes within a reasonable figure."

The flower growers in Carlsbad were the ones most affected by the industrial and residential growth. Until the 1960s the flower industry was Carlsbad's largest employer. Ecke's poinsettias, Frazee's ranunculi, Thompson's roses, Pedley's bird-of-paradise, Hummel's succulents and bromeliads all dominated the local fields and greenhouses, providing employment for many. The farmers were adversely affected in a number of ways including the freeway that paved over fields and increases in tax assessments. During the sixties, agricultural land was classified for tax purposes as potential subdivision land. This classification increased the tax 250 percent between the years 1961 and 1965. Farm delegations protested this assessment classification and requested the land be taxed like any other business or commercial property. When taxes for agricultural land exceeded the total income derived from the land, many Carlsbad growers could no longer afford to farm. Gradually the acres of Carlsbad flower fields were converted into industrial and commercial and residential areas.

Carlsbad's financial stability continued to grow along with the industrial and commercial growth in the city. The largest commercial enterprise developed in the city at this time was the Plaza Camino Real Mall. Built on land deemed worthless for farming, the revenue derived from this multi-million-dollar regional shopping center greatly enhanced Carlsbad's budget. It provided a dependable source of commercial revenue for Carlsbad at a time when the downtown business district was in a financial downturn.

Richard Graves, an expert on

urban redevelopment was consulted on how to revitalize the downtown area of Carlsbad so that it would be a benefit to the city rather than a liability. The construction of Interstate 5 and the mall and the ending of train service all contributed to the overall decline in the downtown business district. Graves suggested a switch from general retail to more specialized shops. He pointed out that in order to entice shoppers into the area, it should be cleaned up and renovated. Graves felt that Carlsbad's climate was perfect for tourism and that the freeway would provide easy access to town. Later in the 1970s, a redevelopment plan was organized and implemented.

Top: *Buena Vista Lagoon looking north to Oceanside, circa 2001.*

Bottom: Buena Vista Lagoon looking north to Oceanside, circa 1989.

Industrial development that began in the sixties occurred on the outermost borders of town. In the northeast area of town the South Coast Asphalt Company established a rock quarry on land that contained the El Salto Falls near the Buena Vista Creek, that feeds water into the Buena Vista Lagoon. In the southeast section of town along Palomar Airport Road, Industrial parks were established. Magnetic Technology, which made precision electric motors, became the first company in the Carlsbad Industrial Park. Numerous other companies were established throughout the area, gradually establishing an industrial corridor along Palomar Airport Road. This industrial development contributed greatly to Carlsbad's financial security and future.

Growing Pains

Carlsbad's territorial growth in the seventies influenced its commercial and residential development then and into the future. The dramatic growth during the seventies, eighties, and nineties contributed to a revolution in lifestyles for Carlsbad residents. Long gone were the days when Carlsbad was a sleepy little

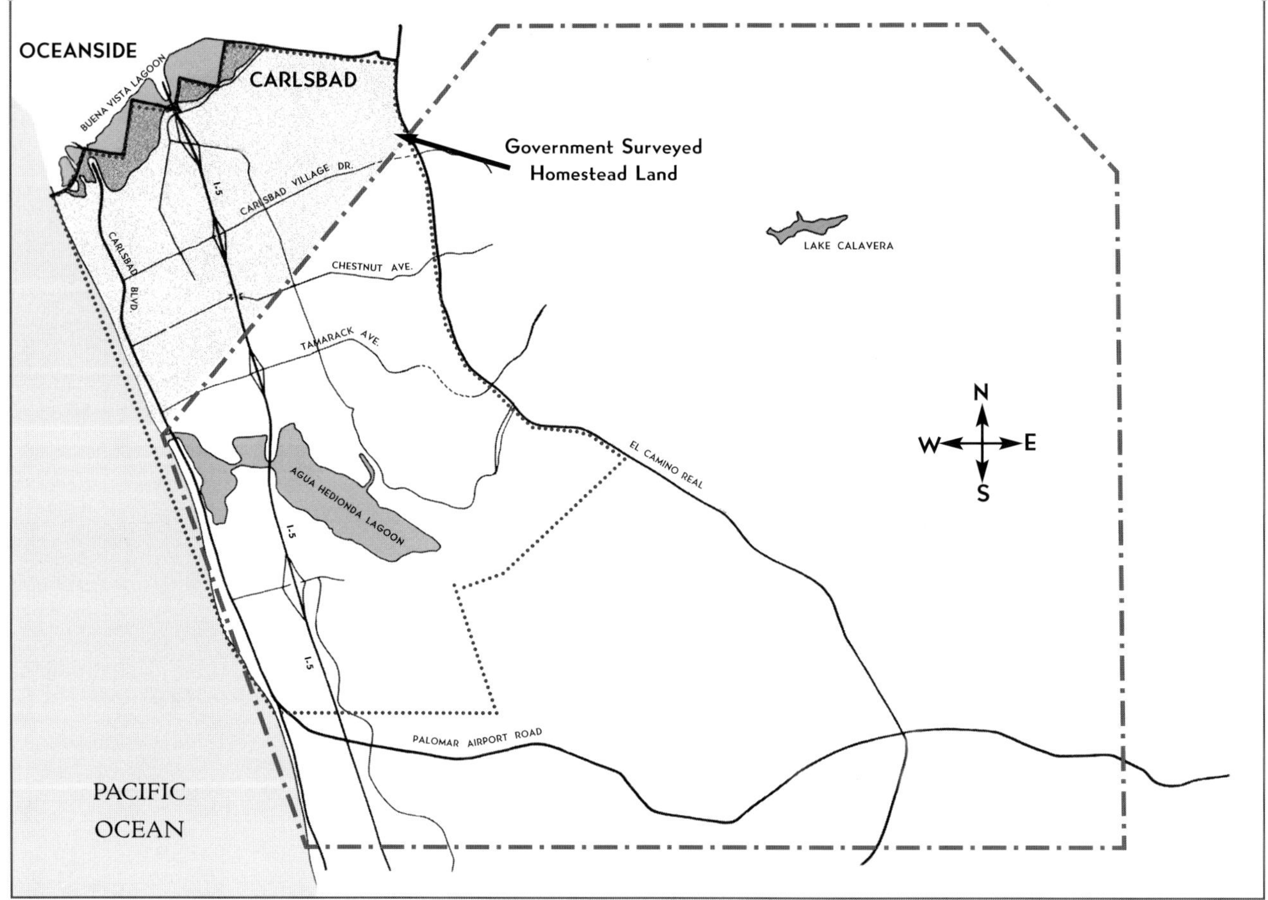

Boundary lines of Rancho Agua Hedionda (dot-dash) and 1952 City of Carlsbad (dotted line).

agricultural town. Carlsbad was transformed into a tourist, residential, and industrial mecca.

Land Annexations

In 1964 Rancho La Costa Inc. developed the La Costa Resort, a country club and spa hotel on the eastern end of the Batiquitos Lagoon. This resort was located just southeast of Carlsbad city borders. Within a few short years, a subsidiary of Rancho La Costa Inc., the La Costa Land Company, began development of a twenty-five-hundred-acre planned community. This development of upscale family homes and condominiums became commonly known as La Costa. Since it was located outside of any incorporated city sphere of influence, the La Costa neighborhood was built and advertised as a resort living development and residents had to shop for basic services such as fire, police, water, and schools. The community chose services from several different providers, picking the ones best suited to their needs.

Dissatisfaction with this system prompted La Costa residents to initiate annexation talks with the city of Carlsbad in 1971. Residents wanted improved fire and police protection, schools, and water and trash service that Carlsbad could provide.

Carlsbad was willing to annex La Costa and Carrillo Ranch,

even though it would mean hiring more city employees and providing more city services. By adding these two separate land holdings, the city's geographical size would expand as well as its tax base. Increases would come from tourism revenue, residential and commercial property taxes, and all future land development.

The Local Agency Formation Commission (LAFCO), an agency established by the State of California, approved the proposed La Costa and Carrillo Ranch annexations to Carlsbad as long as several requirements were met. The first requirement was a petition requesting annexation to Carlsbad signed by at least 25 percent of all registered La Costa voters. After the petition was signed, a public hearing was needed to voice any objections to the annexation. Once the election date was set, approval of annexation would entail 50 percent plus one vote to pass. The last requirement for annexation was that, after the election, the City Council needed to pass an ordinance approving annexation of the proposed land.

The annexation of La Costa and Carrillo Ranch, if approved

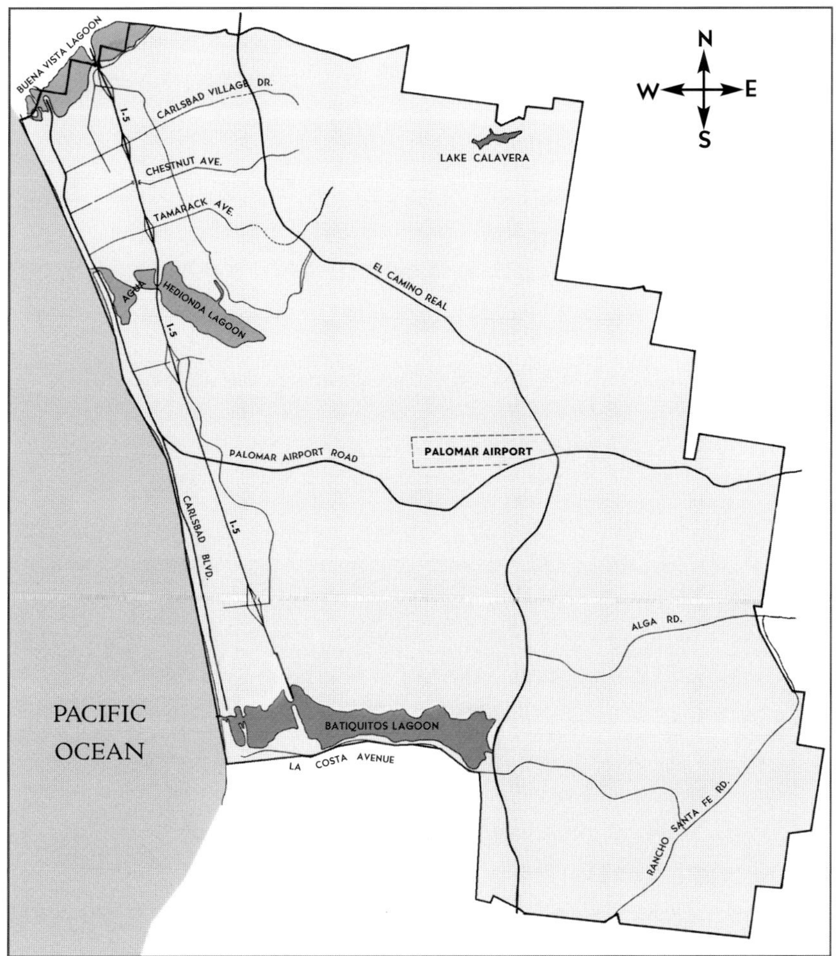

City limits of the City of Carlsbad, 2001.

by the voters, would increase Carlsbad by 5,485 acres or 8.5 square miles. The election, which took place in August 1972 with a 65 percent voter turnout, approved these annexations to Carlsbad with a vote of forty-four in favor and forty against. Once La Costa voters approved the annexation, it was up to the City Council to pass an ordinance accepting the area into the city. La Costa became Carlsbad's southernmost area on October 16, 1972, when annexation documents were filed at the San Diego County Recorder's office.

Carlsbad continued to grow throughout the 1970s and 80s, as bits and pieces of unincorporated county land were gradually annexed to the city. In 1973, LAFCO approved the annexation of 778 acres located near Lake Calavera. In 1978, 186 acres of the Tootsie K Ranch, established by the Kentner family during World War II, were annexed with LAFCO approval. In the same year, LAFCO placed the entire Batiquitos Lagoon and its southern shoreline into Carlsbad's sphere of influence. This was considered a first step towards annexation of the lagoon. While the neighboring community of Leucadia voiced objections to this step, LAFCO justified their action by stating that Carlsbad's status, as an incorporated city, would offer better guardianship of the lagoon's environment and resources. By 1985, Carlsbad had annexed Batiquitos Lagoon, Ponto Beach area, La Costa, Green Valley, land around Palomar Airport, and land east of El Camino Real.

After the Land Annexations

While the land size of the city increased because of the annexations, so did population, housing density, and the city workload. Carlsbad needed to hire more employees, purchase more equipment, build more parks, libraries, fire stations, and provide adequate basic services for these newly acquired areas.

One of the first tasks undertaken after the land annexations was to budget funds for the increased workload. Hiring more employees as building inspectors, policemen, firemen, and public work crews was an immediate priority, since the county had handled all of these services. Establishment of fire stations throughout the larger city was necessary. Likewise, the purchase of equipment for the fire stations and public work crews as well as more police cars were all immediate concerns.

Facing page: Aerial looking east from Terramar to Car Country Carlsbad, circa 1980s.

A second step after land annexations was drafting changes to the Carlsbad General Plan, to determine the necessary amount

of parks, housing, open space, and other facilities and services needed for the future. By 1985, two new elements, the Parks and Recreation and Land Use elements, were added to the General Plan. The Parks and Recreation element established the number of parks and special resource areas needed for the city. It was established that five acres of parkland were needed for every one thousand residents. The second new element was Land Use, and it focused on the need to build public facilities before the developers built new residential units. In 1986 the voters approved a Growth Management Plan that set limits on the number of residential units built, reduced residential density, determined that facilities and services must keep pace with growth, designated 40 percent of city land as open space, and insisted that developers pay their fair share of facilities and services. The Growth Management Plan divided the city into four quadrants. El Camino Real and Palomar Airport Roads were used as the dividing lines for the quadrants. Each quadrant had planning zones, and these zones determined what developers needed to provide before building could begin. Additionally, the Growth Management Plan could not be altered in any way without voter approval.

Aerial looking northeast from La Costa towards Palomar Airport Road, circa 1980s.

Issues Arising from Rapid Development

Rapid development of annexed land and loss of open space created citizen complaints ranging from inadequate services in the newly annexed land to inadequate sewage treatment facilities and the rapid conversion of open space and agricultural land into industrial or residential developments.

A La Costa secession group formed in January 1987, calling themselves the La Costa Town Council. They were frustrated over the La Costa growth management plan, truck traffic on the two-lane Rancho Santa Fe Road, three school districts, and only one representative on City Council. Those who opposed secession pointed out that even though La

Aerial view looking east from ocean entrance to Agua Hedionda Lagoon, circa 1980s.

Costa property contributed greatly to Carlsbad's annual budget, property taxes did not pay for all the services received. At this time a significant amount of the tax base was coming from north of Palomar Airport Road. Additionally, the definition of *La Costa* as being "all of the area south of Palomar Airport Road and east of the freeway" was erroneous. La Costa was only the land developed by the La Costa Land Company, which had sold its remaining undeveloped acres in 1981 to the Daon Corporation. Needless to say, the secession move was fruitless and La Costa remained within Carlsbad city boundaries.

Interestingly enough, one major reason the La Costa Land

Company sold off their undeveloped land, according to their chairman Allard Roen, was frustration over the construction moratorium that had been in effect since 1977. The Carlsbad City Council placed a moratorium on new building in the city because it lacked sufficient sewage treatment capacity.

Residential encroachment on agricultural land caused an avalanche of complaints from citizens pushing for slow growth. Farmers responded that they could not afford to farm, since it cost more to farm, with labor costs, supplies, water, pollution controls, and property taxes, than they could make on the land. Perry Lamb who owned land in south Carlsbad wrote to the San Diego Coast Regional Commission in 1977 asking if the purpose of preserving agricultural use along the coast was to preserve agriculture or to preserve open space. Lamb's opinion was that if it was to preserve agriculture, then farmers would need to build greenhouses to produce crops of higher quality in order to make a profit. He pointed out that greenhouses destroyed the look of "open space" just as much as residential development. Allan O. Kelly, whose family arrived in Carlsbad in the 1860s, stated that farming simply didn't earn enough money to pay for all of the land taxes. Kelly explained that he had dry farmed for forty years, just breaking even.

Early 1960s aerial view of downtown Carlsbad before Pio Pico was realigned and Interstate 5 widened.

For years the Coastal Commission tried to preserve coastal farmland by setting up an Agricultural Improvement Fund. Funded by developer's fees and administered by the Resource Conservation District of San Diego County, this fund was used for subsidizing and making improvements on agricultural land. After years of pressure from the city, the Coastal Commission finally lifted restrictions on the farmland and gave permission in 1985 to develop the agricultural land from El Camino Real west to the Ocean and from Tamarack south to Batiquitos Lagoon.

Rise of Industry and Commerce

Residential development in Carlsbad during the seventies and eighties was occurring along the city's northern and southern borders, leaving the midsection along Palomar Airport Road open for industrial and commercial development. Beginning in the 1960s, the land immediately surrounding the airport was restricted through deed covenants for businesses that related to the aircraft industry. Land adjacent to the airport that was zoned agricultural could be used for other industry if the zoning was changed and sewage issues were addressed. Industry was interested in this land since it was vacant, inexpensive at the time, and the airport provided fast service for company travel. International corporations were interested in the Palomar Airport corridor. Mitsui and Company and Mitsui Fudosan Inc. purchased one-half interest in the Palomar Airport Business Park that was constructed in 1975.

Various businesses located in Palomar Airport Industrial corridor.

Major corporations established businesses in Carlsbad. Two of these were Burroughs, a maker of circuit boards used in computers, and Sargent Industries Stillman Seal Division, a maker of O-rings.

Various businesses located in Palomar Airport Industrial corridor.

Over a community group's objection, San Diego Gas and Electric Company expanded the Encina power plant. SDG&E received approval from the Carlsbad City Council in March 1976 to construct a fifth generating unit and to build a four-hundred-foot stack. The Community Cause group tried to have the California Supreme Court force the city of Carlsbad to hold an election on the Encina expansion. At the same time, SDG&E was planning on a feasibility study for building a refinery in Macario Canyon. By November 1976, an agreement of sorts was reached. The Community Cause group dropped their objections to the Encina expansion and SDG&E dropped their plans for a feasibility study in Macario Canyon.

A variety of smaller commercial and industrial enterprises took hold during this period. Morey Boogie Board Company was started in 1975 on Oak Street. The original boogie board was named after Tom Morey. Morey and his partner, Germain Saive, opened their factory with an investment of $250.

In 1977, the multimillion-dollar Car Country Carlsbad was established. This fifty-acre site of car dealerships contributed enough sales tax money to equal 25 percent of the city's share of residential property tax money. Car dealers formerly located in Oceanside joined together to invest and develop the property. The reason behind their investment was simply lack of space in Oceanside. Many of the dealerships were located in several different buildings along what was then known as Hill Street.

Hubbs Seaworld Research Institute located on Agua Hedionda Lagoon.

Traffic and parking made it difficult for dealers to properly show their inventory. By moving to Carlsbad the dealerships increased income, provided an easier shopping experience for consumers, and had a huge impact on Carlsbad's revenues.

In 1995, the Hubbs Seaworld Research Institute opened on Agua Hedionda Lagoon. As the only Marine Fish Hatchery on the West Coast, this 22,000-square-foot facility produces more than 350,000 juvenile white sea bass a year. Funded by recreational sportfishing licenses, this research institute does studies on the effects of food sources, water quality, and water velocity on the growth and performance of fish. This facility, along with other educational facilities, such as the Gemological Institute, point to Carlsbad's growth outside of business for revenue sources.

The golfing industry also gained a major foothold in Carlsbad with Taylor Made and Calloway Golf manufacturers establishing businesses and production plants along the Palomar Airport corridor. At one point, Callaway Golf became Carlsbad's largest private employer.

Development of all types of industries continued along the industrial corridor on Palomar Airport Road throughout the 1990s. Growth in the business industry spurred a rise in hotel, investment, and educational industries. Industry also helped make Carlsbad a tourist destination, as people came to town on business and stayed for pleasure.

Various businesses located in Palomar Airport Industrial corridor.

Rise of Tourism

Avocado Days that began in the 1920s was Carlsbad's first effort to attract tourists. The grand opening of the California Carlsbad Mineral Spring Hotel in 1930 helped open the

door for tourism by promoting an interest in Carlsbad's mineral water. Throughout the decades that followed, money from tourism continued to contribute to Carlsbad's financial stability. The Twin Inns, with its famous chicken dinners, was reported in a variety of travel magazines, even *National Geographic*. The Royal Palms Motel, and its famous wedding chapel, where it was rumored Claudette Colbert married, was a destination for many who wanted a vacation by the sea. Tourism took a big leap forward when the annexation of La Costa brought the La Costa Resort with its golfing and tennis championships.

Various businesses located in Palomar Airport Industrial corridor.

Tourism and Downtown Redevelopment

The decline in the downtown area prompted the City Council to create a redevelopment agency in 1976. Redevelopment slowly converted the business district into a tourist friendly area and tourism boomed in Carlsbad. A redevelopment plan was adopted in 1981 that included closing disreputable bars; moving auto repair shops from key commercial areas to less visible sites; remodeling storefronts, improving traffic circulation; parking and utilities; and attracting upscale motels, vacation resorts, retail shops, and restaurants. By 1985 the downtown area had improved sufficiently to warrant the establishment of a Carlsbad Convention and Visitors Bureau. This office was sponsored by the Carlsbad Chamber of Commerce and helped by city funds. In 1988, the first of the redevelopment agency bonds issued raised $12 million for downtown projects. Plans for the bond money included a senior citizens complex, parking lots, a pedestrian promenade along the sea, streetscapes that would widen the streets, and new sidewalks, gutters, and traffic lights.

One of the first efforts to foster interest in the downtown area took place in 1975, when Buddy Storms organized the Village Faire. Originating as a sidewalk sale for a small group of vendors who sold garage sale items downtown, the Street Faire slowly grew during subsequent decades. By the 1990s, under the direction of Keith Kennedy, the semiannual Village Faire was bringing thousands of tourists into town.

The Carlsbad Triathlon began in 1981. This race includes a one-mile ocean swim, sixteen-mile bike ride, and a 6.2-mile run and brings athletes from all over the world.

Establishment of the Carlsbad 5000 Race in 1986 also drew tourists to town. The 5,000-meter road race took advantage of the newly redeveloped downtown area, starting at the corner of Jefferson Street and Grand Avenue and racing through town.

In 1988 the City Council approved construction of the sixty-nine-thousand-square-foot Village Faire, a shopping center built downtown just a few blocks from the ocean. This shopping center became a cornerstone for the tourism industry in downtown Carlsbad. The combination of restaurants and shops and live music draws tourists into this shopping area close to their hotels and timeshares.

Tourism expanded outside of the downtown area in 1993, when the flower fields along Interstate 5 were converted from an agricultural endeavor to a business, where growing flowers was just one element. The Carltas Company, the land management division of the Ecke family, secured a loan from the California Coastal Conservancy to establish the Flower Fields at Carlsbad Ranch. The Flower Fields, planted with

Before and after construction of Carlsbad Country Stores, early 1990s and 2001. (Futrell Collection)

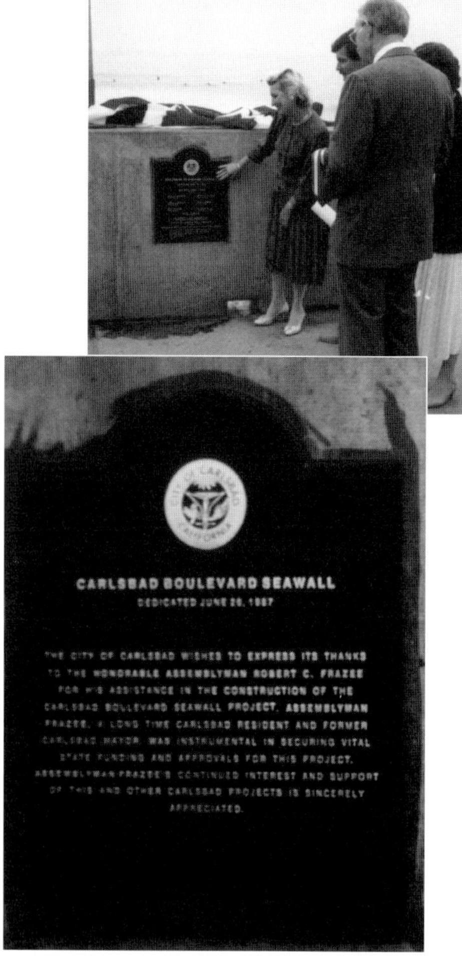

Seawall dedication along Carlsbad Boulevard, 1986–87.

Below right: Boys Club and Wonder Bread Bakery in downtown Carlsbad.

ranunculi, draw two hundred thousand paying visitors a year to walk among the rows of flowers on sixty acres that overlook the ocean. A 1999 University of California Cooperative Extension Study found that these visitors spend over $2.3 million dollars a year in Carlsbad and over $7.8 million dollars in San Diego County.

Tourists have come to Carlsbad for over thirty years to play golf. The La Costa Resort has two PGA Championship courses that allow golfers to measure their ability against the worlds best. The development of the four star Aviara Golf Course in 1991, which overlooks the Batiquitos Lagoon, brought more tourism dollars into the City of Carlsbad.

In 1999, Legoland opened just a few miles away from the Flower Fields. Before this Danish-owned theme park was built in Carlsbad it faced stiff opposition. NAIL, Neighbors Against the Invasion of Lego, was a community group that opposed Legoland moving to Carlsbad. Arguments against Lego's construction included increased traffic, a burden on city services, overcrowding at beaches, and a deterioration of lifestyle. Lego's rebuttal focused on the fact that the 128-acre park would generate less traffic than the Plaza Camino Real Mall, which was located on the same amount of land. In June 1994 citizens agreed to the construction of Lego in Carlsbad with a 57 percent approval vote. Legoland opened in March of 1999.

The National Association of Music Makers opened the Museum of Making Music in March 2000.

The museum, with over 450 instruments in its collection and five displays that span the years 1890 to 1990, has become a definite draw for those tourists who are musically inclined.

Top: New businesses along Faraday.

Above: The Island at Faraday.

Government Meets Community Needs

While the rapid rise in industry, commerce, tourism, and residential development continued for three decades, city government needed to find ways to enhance the quality of life of Carlsbad residents. As early as 1983, the city began a program that provided community garden space for residents who had no space of their own. The garden program was implemented under the direction of Doug Duncanson, with the lifestyle of the apartment dweller or senior citizen in mind.

Knowing of the demand for library services to meet the needs of a growing population, the City Council purchased land in 1987 for a future city library to be located in La Costa. The 64,000-square-foot building opened on September 25, 1999, and was almost three times larger than the first library built on Elm Avenue in 1967.

After two years of negotiations, an agreement was reached between the City of Carlsbad and the Carlsbad Unified School District that facilitated the building of a Senior Center and new School District Offices on the old Pine School site. The city built a 28,300-square-foot building that housed both the Senior Center and School District offices. After the building opened in 1989, the city leased the office space to the district for a period of ten years, at which time the School District received condominium ownership of its share of the building.

In 1989, the city finally realized a long-term goal to take over control of the water district. Receiving LAFCO approval in June 1989, the Costa Real Municipal Water District officially became the Carlsbad Municipal Water District on January 1, 1990. The directors of the Water District were to stay on as commissioners, however, almost all authority was turned over to the city.

Grand opening of Senior Center / Carlsbad Unified School District offices.

In an effort to meet the needs of marginalized residents, the city implemented a hiring hall for migrant workers. Operating on leased county land, the Carlsbad Hiring Center opened in July 1991. The Center, by providing a meeting place for workers and employers, removed many of the laborers who congregated on street corners.

In 1993 the city also offered support for a Catholic Charities project called La Posada de Guadalupe de Carlsbad. Conceived as a shelter for homeless workers, state grant money was used to build and operate a dormitory where those in need could stay for three months, while attending job workshops and looking for employment.

Chestnut Street Pumpkin Patch, late 1980s.

Right: Chestnut Street Pumpkin Patch, 2001.

In response to citizen concerns over the natural environment, the city adopted a Habitat Management Plan in 1999. The intent was to set aside sixty-five-hundred acres of natural habitat that would retain the open space necessary for protection of endangered and indigenous species. By including natural corridors that connect one area with another through industrial and residential areas, the Habitat Management Plan hopes to retain a viable and natural lifestyle the endangered species in Carlsbad.

Carlsbad's growth has effected lifestyle changes for humans as well as animals. Considering the rise in residential, industrial, and commercial development in the past thirty years, Carlsbad's agricultural identity is almost gone. It will be interesting to see what changes the next thirty years will bring to the city.

Hummel's Exotic Gardens

When E. C. Hummel, a leading bromeliad grower, moved his nursery to Carlsbad from Los Angeles in 1952, he was quoted as saying "Carlsbad is a place where a nursery might have a few years of life before being crowded out by real estate subdivisions." Carlsbad's climate, soil, and open space drew the

Hummels to town in the early 1950s, just as it had drawn growers since 1916.

E. C. Hummel was not well known in Carlsbad even though he was one of the leading bromeliad growers in the United States. He concentrated more on his work than on local affairs and became very well known nationally and internationally. His nursery, with hybridization of new euphorbia variations, bromeliads, and succulents, became a mecca for the unusual and distinctive. Hummel worked with his wife to develop new hybrids and was a contributing author to university textbooks on the care and growing of exotic plants.

Upon his retirement in the early 1970s, most of the plants in Hummel's Exotic Gardens were sold off. The Missouri Botanical Gardens established a permanent display of Hummel's hybrids and they were viewed as the finest produced in America at that time. Hummel shipped plants to the San Diego Wild Animal Park, Missouri Botanical Gardens, the Milwaukee County Park Horticultural Conservatory, the Sydney Opera House Gardens in Australia, and Huntington Gardens in San Marino. Today, the location of Hummel's Exotic Gardens on Park Drive is now a housing subdivision.

Mr. and Mrs. E. C. Hummel at their Park Drive nursery.

CHAPTER 10

Police and Fire Departments

Police Department

Carlsbad's Police Department began in October 1952, when Max Palkowski was hired as the city's first police chief. Only thirty-two years old when he assumed the responsibility of being Carlsbad's one-man police force, he was credited with handling people well and with a sense of humor. He worked many hours of overtime, even placing a siren on top of his own car to convert it into the city police car. When asked why he wanted to work as a police officer, he replied, "There is no heavy lifting."

Chief Palkowski put together the nucleus of the police force picking his staff from the police reserves on the recommendations of his regular police officers. In his opinion, exams were the worst way to choose police officers since they didn't tell you how well they worked with others. The reserve police officers made it possible for Carlsbad's Police Department to function at a basic level until the city could afford to hire full-time officers.

Palkowski's work ethic and personality were so greatly appreciated by the city that he was appointed city manager from November 1958 through 1959 to combat the low morale of city employees during this time. He resigned the post at the end of 1959 and resumed his job as police chief saying that his time as city manager was a miserable time for him personally. Palkowski felt that he was not professionally equipped to do the job and that in his heart he always wanted to be a police officer. It was Chief Palkowski who permitted the construction of the Carlsbad Raceway. He was the only police chief in San Diego County who would approve locating the raceway in their own town. Palkowski said, "I don't think many people realize that the people of professional quality are the heart of the sport." Chief Palkowski remained in his position until retirement in 1970.

Fire Department's annual Christmas Village in 1966.

Top: Carlsbad's first new police car was a 1953 Ford.

Middle: Alliss Eunnis, Max Palkowski, and Natalie Vermilyea.

Bottom: Police Chief Max Palkowski and other volunteers donated time in 1954 to ready City Hall and the Fire and Police Departments.

Once Carlsbad started a series of land annexations that increased the city's borders, it also meant a change in Carlsbad's police force. An expanded beat patrol meant more officers on the force. Adding La Costa with its specialized golf and tennis championships meant an increase in police protection. In 1952 Carlsbad had one sworn officer, by 1971 it had increased to ten sworn officers, and by 1981 there were fifty-four officers.

Every increase in the police force added to overcrowding the office space. The first Police Department, located in the old Saint Patrick's Church, moved in 1954 to a new building on Pio Pico and Elm Avenue, which it shared with the Fire Department and City Hall. In 1968, when Interstate 5 was widened, the City Hall was rebuilt facing a realigned Pio Pico Drive and the Police Department continued to share a building with other city offices. As city government continued to grow, office space at this site shrunk. The Police Department was moved into a variety of portable buildings on the grounds of City Hall, while waiting for a new structure to be built in the geographic center of the city. This new facility, known as the Safety Center, opened in 1986 and housed both the Police Department and Fire Department's administrative offices.

The current Carlsbad Police Department has 100 sworn officers, 38 nonsworn officers, and 120 volunteers. The variety of volunteer programs that continue to supplement the Police Department, including reserve officers, in-house personal, juvenile justice panel, and the senior patrol, all demonstrate citizens involvement in the community.

Fire Department

Carlsbad's fire service began as a Volunteer Fire Department in 1952. According to one of the volunteers, about half a dozen men met at the old State Forestry Fire Station on the corner of Beech Avenue and Carlsbad Boulevard. The volunteers studied firefighting on the job and attended classroom training in El Cajon. These classes were sponsored by the California state fire marshal, and were taught by "experts."

The Carlsbad Volunteer Fire Department (CVFD) sponsored barbecues, dances, and other fundraisers in order to raise money to equip the Fire Department. Volunteers assembled the first fire truck, combining a purchased Ford truck chassis with a tank purchased from the Marine Corps at Camp Pendleton. They also used a pump and hard line with reel from the State Forestry Department, and the plumbing from local stores. One of the volunteers explained how the peripheral equipment such as hoses, pry bars, and nozzles was obtained. One of the early volunteers Warren Clark stated, "These costly items proved to be almost impossible to obtain until we came upon the idea that we make ourselves available to roll for assistance to other departments. This was like ordering the fox into the henhouse. By hook, crook, or con job we usually came home to our station with some new piece of something that we needed."

Safety Center "Moving In Day" in 1986.

Below, left: Carlsbad Fire Department.

Bob Hardin, who worked for the Municipal Water Company, also volunteered for the CVFD. He knew the site of all the fireplugs in town and how much pressure each could give. Mrs. Hardin took the calls for CVFD, sounded the siren that called the volunteers to duty, and logged the information on a blackboard. The system worked so well that insurance rates for

Carlsbad homeowners dropped to the same level as those cities with full-time fire departments. The CVFD, which was created out of necessity, worked because of the volunteer spirit of the community.

The City of Carlsbad began the city-funded Fire Department in 1954. The first fire truck was purchased in March, the first full-time fireman, Floyd Hollowell, was hired in October, and in November dedication occurred for the new $19,000 Fire Department and Police Station built at Pio Pico Drive and Elm Avenue. Many of the firemen for the early Fire Department were still volunteers. In order to save money for the city, volunteer firemen, police reserves, and full-time employees did some of the construction and painting for the new building.

Early the next year in 1955, volunteer fireman Bob Hardin was hired as Carlsbad's first fire chief. With an operating budget of $27,000 for the 1955–56 fiscal year efforts of the twenty-one volunteer firemen were greatly needed and appreciated. Volunteers sponsored and ran the yearly Fireman's Ball that was held at the Carlsbad Hotel to raise money for uniforms, firehouse furniture, and related equipment. Chief Hardin continually asked the City Council to increase funding for more paid positions.

Top: Groundbreaking ceremony for Safety Center.

Above: Mayor Casler at groundbreaking ceremony for new Fire Station in La Costa.

As the city grew so did the Fire Department. And one of the earliest causalities of the Fire Department's growth was the abolition of the Christmas Scene in 1969. Begun in 1954, the firemen constructed a winter wonderland in front of their station on Pio Pico Drive. Battalion Chief Alex Wolenchuck and Eddie Garcia worked year after year creating the miniature homes and churches used each year for the Christmas Scene.

Seen by travelers from the freeway, as many as thirty thousand visitors would stop in Carlsbad to view the display. In 1969, Battalion Chief Alex Wolenchuck announced that due to a combination of circumstances, the Christmas Scene would not be displayed. The Interstate 5 freeway expansion, the year before, forced the Fire Department to move from the Pio Pico location, thus reducing the number of visitors to two thousand. Additionally, growth of the Fire Department along with the expansion of the city meant that crews were too busy with their paid jobs as firefighters to take time each year building and maintaining the Christmas Scene.

In 1972, La Costa was annexed to the City of Carlsbad, thus increasing the responsibilities for the Carlsbad Fire Department. In 1973, the city had two fire stations, one on Arenal and the other on Elm Avenue. The Fire Department also responded to calls from unincorporated land called "donut holes," areas surrounded by the city. Many of the firemen at this time had originally worked as volunteer firemen under Bob Hardin, before being hired on as full-time employees. As firemen were hired into the department, a rule was implemented that they had to live within twelve miles of the city center, which was considered the corner of El Camino Real and Palomar Airport Road.

As the Fire Department grew so did its professionalism.

El Camino Real is in right-hand corner of this photo of residential development in the early 1980s.

Under direction of Fire Chief Jim Thompson, Carlsbad developed a fire sprinkler ordinance for commercial buildings. Also, a non-combustible roof ordinance, the first of its kind in San Diego County, was sponsored by Chief Thompson. Also during this period, an Emergency Operations Center was set up and the emergency preparedness plan was rewritten. Chief Thompson, who served from 1976 to 1992, improved Carlsbad Fire Department services so much that Carlsbad's fire defenses classification dropped from Class 6 to Class 4. This reduction in classification meant that Carlsbad residents actually paid less in fire protection insurance premiums.

Intersection of El Camino and Palomar Airport Road looking east, circa 1980.

Smoke from the fire at Harmony Grove loomed upon the horizon, looking south from East Pointe Drive in the northwest quadrant at 5:30 p.m.

Carlsbad Fire Department crews faced the biggest fire in Carlsbad's history in October 1996. This fast moving fire was named the "Harmony Grove Fire," since it is believed the fire originated in the Harmony Grove area. It destroyed fifty-four homes. Forty-eight of the homes destroyed had wood shake roofs. After the fire, the City Council adopted an ordinance that prohibited all but Class A noncombustible roofs.

Today the Carlsbad Fire Department is an entirely different entity from the one begun in 1952 as a volunteer organization. While this Fire Department does coordinate with other cities in case of fire, it also provides paramedic services, holds fire prevention demonstrations, inspects for fire code compliance, and presents firesafety classes for children. Seventy-three firefighters and officers are now located throughout the city and staff six fire stations. ❧

Below, left and right: The remains of the destruction at Harmony Grove, several weeks after the fire.

CHAPTER II

Library Services and Arts Office

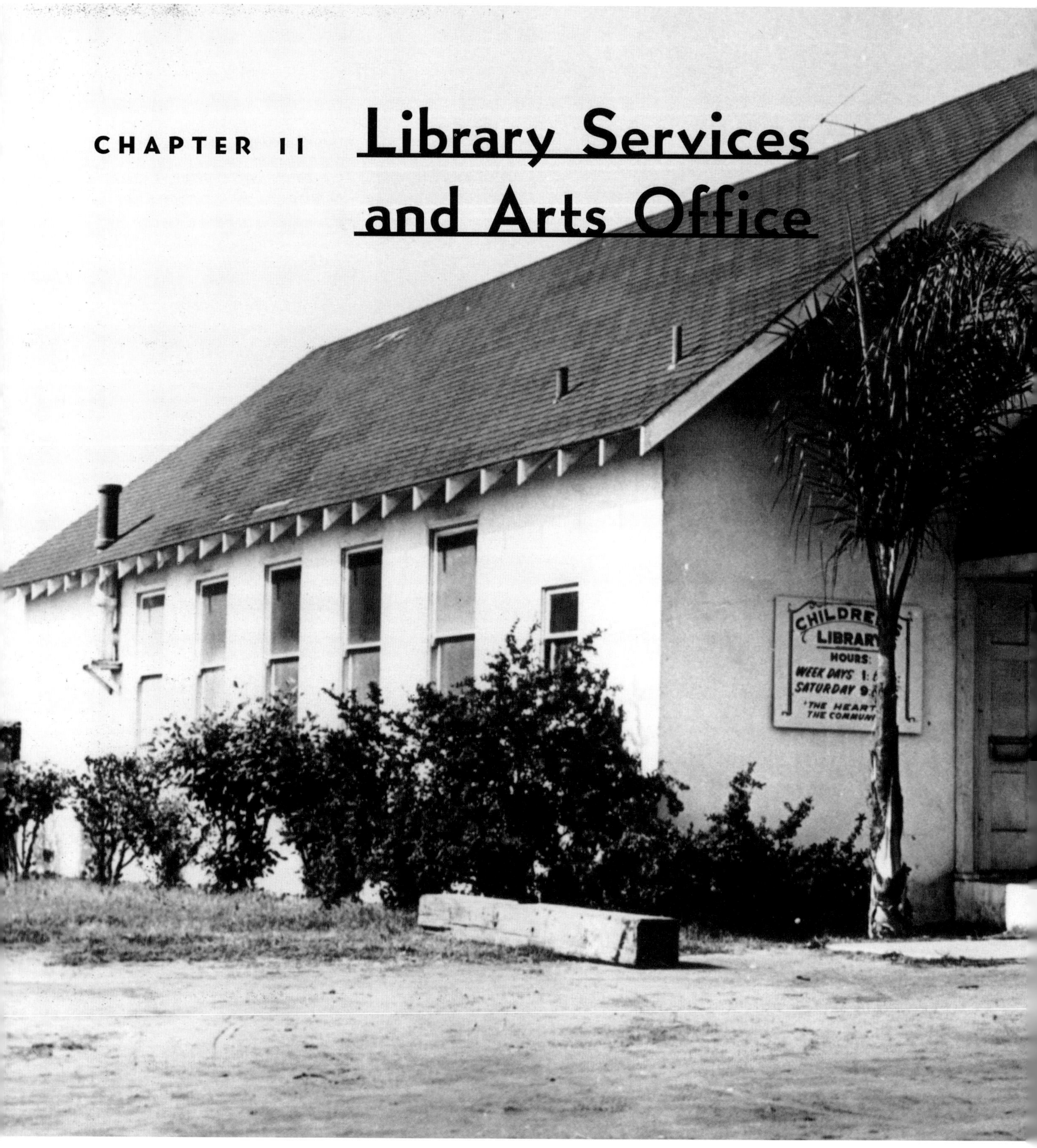

Library

Carlsbad has had some form of library service since 1916, when San Diego County established a small County Library on one shelf of Simpson's Dry Goods Store. In 1926, the County "Library Shelf" moved to Chase's Store. By 1931, the *Carlsbad Journal* offices donated three shelves for County Library services. A list of recently received books would appear each week in the newspaper. The Library remained in the newspaper offices until 1953, when it was moved to a corner of old Saint Patrick's Church on Harding Street. At the same time, the county sent a librarian to work part time in the Carlsbad Branch Library. Georgina Cole, the county branch librarian, shared the Harding Street address with the newly formed Carlsbad Police Department. In 1956, the city established its own Library System, appointing Georgina Cole as Carlsbad's first library director.

Carlsbad's first Library, the former Saint Patrick's Church, is now located in Magee Park and is known as Heritage Hall.

Formation of the Library was a community effort. Local clubs and residents donated shelves, furniture, telephones, books, and cash towards the new Library. Georgina Cole donated a large number of books from her personal library to supplement Carlsbad's collection.

In 1958, the adult collection needed more space and was moved to a section of the Carlsbad Mutual Water Company office building at the corner of Elm and Roosevelt. The Children's Library was located in a separate building, strapping staff resources as they moved back and forth between the two buildings during the day.

Carlsbad's Elm Avenue Library, built in 1967, was named in honor of Georgina Cole, the city's first library director, in 1999.

Below, right: Carlsbad City Library established Centro de Información which opened in 1991 to integrate Spanish-speaking residents into the general community.

Georgina Cole organized a group of library supporters in 1963. Calling themselves The Friends of the Library, they promoted a successful bond campaign that financed construction of a new twenty-four-thousand-square-foot Library on Elm Avenue. In 1967, the spacious building opened, housing a book collection of 47,699 volumes.

Since then the services and resources of Carlsbad's Library System have continued to grow. In 1976, the Rambling Reader Book Mobile was started. It was used as an outreach tool to provide library services to the newly annexed La Costa area in South Carlsbad. In 1984, a Library branch was opened for the first time in La Costa and the Rambling Reader ceased to function.

This is one of the first TGIF Jazz in the Parks Programs staged at Magee Park.

In 1990, the Library received a five-year $40,000 "Federal Partnerships for Change" grant. This grant enabled the Library to create a program specifically designed to integrate Spanish-speaking residents into the larger community. In 1991, the Centro de Información opened in a Pine School classroom. The program was so successful that it received the League of California Cities Helen Putnam Award for Outstanding Achievement in 1994.

Throughout the 1990s, the Library infrastructure was updated and computerized. The card catalog was computerized to provide online research capabilities. In 1999, a new sixty-four-thousand-square-foot Library was opened in South Carlsbad. The $18-million facility included an art gallery, children's library, and auditorium. In April 2000, Robert Gartner, donated $100,000 for the purchase of a limited-edition Steinway Art Case grand piano for the Ruby G. Schulman Auditorium. The same month, April 2000, after the original Elm Avenue Library was remodeled, it reopened as the Georgina Cole Library. In addition to offering the usual library services, the Cole Library specializes in genealogical and local history resources. Forty-four years after the Carlsbad Library System was established, it was recently ranked tenth best in the nation in the 50,000–100,000 population category.

The 64,000-square-foot Dove Library, the newest addition to Carlsbad's Library System, opened in 1999.

Arts Office

One of Carlsbad's most noticeable community-oriented programs is the Arts Office. Established in 1986 by a city ordinance, it was formed to promote and develop public awareness of the arts in Carlsbad. One of the most frequented and well loved of all programs sponsored by the Arts Office is the TGIF Jazz in the Parks summer concert series. Every Friday evening from mid-June to mid-August, a jazz concert is held in one of the Carlsbad parks. The program that began in the late 1980s with one park and about three hundred attendees now has four venues with an average of three thousand attending. Besides jazz concerts, the Arts Office sponsors cultural events as well as public art displays located throughout the city. ❧

This plaque honoring landscaper Ralph Wrisley is located at the small park on Camino Vida Roble.

Below: Ralph Wrisley, Pat Hatfield, and John Futrell designing and planting atrium at Cole Library.

CHAPTER 12 Travel Connections

Roads

Successful development and growth of a town occur when one has easy access to the area. A variety of transportation modes brought people into Carlsbad by road, train, and air. The importance of roads cannot be overlooked, as they are fundamental in allowing access into and out of an area. The first documented account of land travel comes from the 1769 Crespi-Portola records. The Spanish exploration team walked north, along a preexisting trail on the eastern side of Carlsbad's three lagoons. Originally made by Native Americans and later improved on by the Spanish, Californios, and early American settlers, the trail followed the upper ridgelines on the coastal hills. Staying on the high ground facilitated travel by eliminating severe erosion. Bits and pieces of this trail became El Camino Real and it was Carlsbad's first road. During the Rancho days, El Camino Real provided the only north-south land transportation route for travelers, passing through Rancho Agua Hedionda. What is believed to be Carlsbad's first home, the Kelly Adobe, was constructed between 1842 and 1853 by Juan Maria Marron and was located close to El Camino Real. Once rail lines were established, El Camino Real played an important role in train service. Stagecoaches traveled the road daily bringing passengers to the coastal train depots. El Camino Real remained a simple oiled dirt road up to the late 1940s. After Camp Pendleton was established north of Carlsbad, the Marine Corps advocated for improvements on El Camino Real. The Marine Corps wanted two land routes connecting their base to San Diego. Prior to the 1940s, Highway 101 was the only road running all the way from San Diego to Los Angeles. Often, coastal weather conditions obscured visibility on Highway 101 and slow-moving traffic caused congestion. Road widening and paving began along El Camino Real from the northern border of Vista Way south to Palomar Airport Road.

This is Coast Highway, also known as Carlsbad Boulevard, south of Tamarack, circa 1930. (Courtesy San Diego Historical Society)

Coast Highway/Carlsbad Boulevard, south of Tamarack, circa 2001.

Below, right: The California Carlsbad Hotel that opened in 1930 was built on the 1927 Coast Highway.

In the late 1960s, construction began on the Plaza Camino Real Shopping Center, located at the intersection of El Camino Real and Highway 78. San Diego County and the City of Carlsbad undertook a joint project widening the two-lane El Camino Real to four lanes in anticipation of future mall traffic.

Between 1970 and 2000 a tremendous amount of development and construction occurred along El Camino Real. Housing subdivisions, shopping centers, and business parks gradually replaced the agricultural fields running along either side of the road. Increased traffic and congestion on El Camino Real, traveling to and from the business parks highlighted the road's importance for the economic welfare of Carlsbad and its regional neighbors.

Highway 101, or Carlsbad Boulevard as it is called running through town, is another road that had a significant impact on the city. Running north to south along the coastline, it was the first road that directly connected Carlsbad to San Diego in the south and Oceanside in the north. In Carlsbad, the road originally known as Lincoln Street was changed to Carlsbad Boulevard when the state of California realigned the Coast Highway in 1927. It was just twelve years earlier in 1915, that the Coast Road was paved and the old wooden bridge over the Buena Vista Lagoon was replaced by a concrete structure.

The realignment of Lincoln/Carlsbad Boulevard along with the construction of a railroad overpass caused considerable concern within the Carlsbad Business District. Through traffic now bypassed the State Street business district. Business owners feared the street "diversion gave visitors little opportunity to view the 'real' town" (*Carlsbad Journal*, 1927). However, rather than adversely affecting business, the street realignment spurred the establishment of several new enterprises. In the late 1920s, The Shade a Sea Auto Inn, The Red Apple, and The Carlsbad Mineral Spring Hotel were constructed along the newly realigned Carlsbad Boulevard.

Carlsbad's appeal as a tourist destination began with the construction of new businesses on Carlsbad Boulevard.

Cheryl Jandros riding her horse on El Camino Real near the present-day Plaza Camino Real Mall, circa late 1940s. (Courtesy Jandros Collection)

Interior of the California Carlsbad Mineral Spring Hotel, circa 1930. (Courtesy of the San Diego Historical Society)

The Carlsbad Mineral Spring Hotel that opened in 1930 brought celebrities to Carlsbad throughout the Depression years. They came to the hotel to rest, partake in mineral baths, and to participate in Dr. P. M. Seixas's exercise programs broadcast in the evenings on radio station KNX from the Buena Vista Lagoon. The restorative affects of mineral baths brought baseball teams such as the Padres, who sent their pitchers and catchers to Carlsbad for preliminary

This map shows First Street prior to the realignment of Lincoln Street.

Below: Old Highway 78, west from present-day College. (Courtesy the Hayes Marron Collection)

spring training. Padres' owner H. W. Lane highly recommended Carlsbad to all ball teams, stating that the climate, the baths, and the hotel accommodations created the ideal spot for spring training. This constituted a major change in focus for the city. Rather than being just a place known for its agriculture, the concept of Carlsbad as a final vacation destination took hold.

Established places like the Twin Inns Restaurant also prospered from the newly realigned Coast Highway. The increase in tourism warranted construction of a larger dining room at the Twin Inns.

Prior to 1952 the Carlsbad Chamber of Commerce, acting as a de facto government, sought solutions from appropriate government agencies of San Diego County or California state government to solve local problems. While State Street and Carlsbad Boulevard were paved in 1935, most of the other streets in town were dirt roads. The Chamber asked John Cole, San Diego County's road superintendent, to implement a State Emergency Relief Association program so that six miles of Carlsbad roads could be graded and oiled. Oiling streets lowered their maintenance costs and protected valuable trees and crops from harmful clouds of dust. In the downtown area streets were gradually paved and sewer lines laid.

Three years later, in 1938, the Carlsbad Chamber submitted another petition to the San Diego County Board of Supervisors to change several street names. At this time County Avenue became Basswood and County Road became Chestnut.

The Chamber of Commerce made a major effort to beautify city streets. Renowned

This map shows the 1927 realignment of Lincoln Street to Coast Highway / Carlsbad Boulevard.

horticulturist Kate Sessions often spoke to Carlsbad groups such as the Woman's Club and the Chamber of Commerce. During the 1920s and '30s she offered expert advice on which trees and plants would do well in the coastal climate. Massive plantings of avocados, subtropical fruit trees, and eucalyptus dominated Carlsbad streets, lagoons, and hillsides. Trees abounded around Buena Vista and Agua Hedionda Lagoons, as well as on Highland and Chestnut. Tree planting made the city more visually appealing and attracted tourists and investors.

An abundance of trees became one of Carlsbad's most notable features. Elm Avenue was a tunnel of eucalyptus trees from Carlsbad Boulevard to Highland, planted in 1886 by the Carlsbad Land and Water Company. The trees on Elm Avenue were removed when state funds became available for street improvements in 1955. The increased traffic on Elm, due to the newly constructed Interstate-5 freeway off-ramp, made the street improvements necessary. Citizens protested the removal of their beloved trees, stating, "without beautiful trees we would be just another ordinary little town" (Greenwood, *Carlsbad Journal*, 1955). However, the California State Department of Highways adamantly insisted that the "State Gas Tax Money" slated for the Elm Avenue improvements could only be used when the road width increased from twenty feet to forty feet. This road expansion could not be accomplished by retaining the trees. Carlsbad's financially strapped government could not afford sentimentality and the trees were removed.

Elm Avenue/Carlsbad Village Drive prior to streetscape (top); Elm Avenue/Carlsbad Village Drive after streetscape.

Interstate 5 was the third and last north-south road running through Carlsbad. A 10.7-mile section of this highway was constructed between Carlsbad and Oceanside in 1953 and by 1966 a 25-mile stretch between La Costa Avenue south to San Diego was completed. Interstate 5 brought immense change to Carlsbad. The freeway bisected the city and forced the realignment of roads such as Pio Pico, which meant moving City Hall and Fire Station No. 1 and dealt a blow to the downtown business district. Before Interstate 5 opened, traffic on Highway 101 (Carlsbad Boulevard) averaged fifty-five thousand cars a day. Volume dropped to seven thousand in 1966. However, just as the 1927 realignment of Carlsbad Boulevard created new businesses, the construction of Interstate 5 also created new business opportunities. Interstate 5 increased accessibility to the city for tourists and local residents.

After Carlsbad incorporated in 1952, oversight of neighborhood street development and maintenance was transferred from

San Diego County to the city. Curbs, sidewalks, and street widening took place throughout town. Improvements on Roosevelt, undertaken in 1959, used funds from the 1911 Street Acts.

The city implemented a street naming policy in 1973, pointing out how easy the new system was for locating an address. When the city annexed La Costa, the growth in city boundaries made the implementation of an easier street naming system necessary, so that a street could be located in an emergency situation. The first part of the system was naming a street based on its location in one of seven predetermined city areas. Each of these seven areas of the city was assigned a name designation of an animal, a famous person, a flower, tree, bird, a Spanish name, or a topographical characteristic, as long as it

Top: Prior to Tamarack Street widening project, 1992 (left); After Tamarack Street widening project, 1992 (right).

Bottom: Corner of Pine and Carlsbad Boulevard, 1986–87, prior to Art Park construction.

Carlsbad Boulevard Bluff-top Promenade, 1988.

did not conflict with a preexisting name. The total name with spaces included could not exceed seventeen spaces, in order to fit in street signs. The designation following the name: Street, Drive, Paseo, or Avenue, indicated if the street ran north-south or east-west, or if it was straight or curvy. However this policy was only for newly constructed roads and was not retroactive.

In 1976 the Chamber of Commerce suggested that the city change Elm to Carlsbad Village Drive, which violated the seventeen-character maximum rule. Changing Elm Avenue to Carlsbad Village was suggested as a way to encourage tourism into the downtown area, which was suffering from the I-5 road diversion in 1966 and from the 1968 opening of the Plaza Camino Real Mall. The Carlsbad City Planning Department pointed out two potential problems with changing the name: confusion with the already existing Carlsbad Boulevard and the cost of changing the Interstate-5 signs. More than ten years later, in 1987, the City Council endorsed the name change, estimating the actual cost of street sign changes to be $5,000. However, they did not consider that the name changes on I-5 freeway signs would

Beginning seawall construction, 1986–87, at Tamarack Beach parking lot.

Carlsbad Boulevard Bluff-top Promenade, 1988.

increase from a standard sixteen feet to twenty-six feet, increasing the cost to $143,000!

From the late 1970s through the early 1990s the city implemented a series of improvements to provide a safer road system in Carlsbad for both drivers and pedestrians. Street improvements entailed elimination of street parking on Elm. Diagonal parking changed to parallel parking on Carlsbad Boulevard and parking lots were added on Roosevelt and State Streets. More off-street parking made driving easier and safer. In 1989 massive road improvements along Carlsbad Boulevard included seawall walks, a wider road, and better bridges, all of which enhanced the enjoyment of the Pacific Ocean, one of Carlsbad's most treasured resources.

Sometimes street improvements, with safety in mind, conflict with aesthetic considerations. So far, the city has tried to find a balance that complements functionality and beauty.

Trains

In 1881, Robert Kelly gave the Southern California Railway permission to lay a rail line through his Rancho Agua Hedionda property. Before this time, those who arrived or departed or simply passed through Rancho Agua Hedionda had to do so on foot, by horse, oxcart, or wagon. John Kelly's narrative, "Life on a

These people are watching a train cross over Buena Vista Lagoon, prior to 1910.

San Diego County Ranch," detailed his family's 1868 trip to their Los Kiotes homestead by wagon from San Diego. He said that it took a full day to travel from San Diego to Carlsbad. The oxcart that was carrying the household goods took two days to travel the same distance. The travel time involved before the arrival of trains was dependent on road conditions or what was hauled in wagons or by herding.

Rail service provided new opportunities for those who were already living in the area. Train travel meant they could go to and from San Diego in a matter of hours, no longer making it an all-day journey. It gave them greater accessibility to the outside world and opened up a wealth of opportunities: easier travel, an influx of new people, and new forms of employment. People could easily move to Carlsbad to engage in businesses other than ranching. They could undertake enterprises such as commercial farming that depended on getting crops to market before they spoiled. If the school system was not adequate, they could send their children to a larger city. Residents realized the train was a convenient mode of transportation.

While early rail service was a boon to the local population, it was also unreliable and unpredictable. Trains did not always stop at a station. W. W. Borden reported in the July 1886 edition of the *Plain Truth* newspaper, "It is easy to hear the Cannonball train arriving since it sounds like thunder." This was a good tip for his readers, because passengers often needed to flag the train down in order for it to stop. Sometimes they would set a small brush fire on the tracks to alert the train engineer. The cattle guard on the front of the train would disperse the burning material. Those waiting passengers would stomp out the fire and get onboard.

Carlsbad Train Depot was briefly known as "Carl," circa 1907.

Several station stops built along the rail lines north and south of Rancho Agua Hedionda served the outlying ranches and inland towns. The largest of these stations eventually became the Carlsbad Depot, built just beyond Rancho Agua Hedionda's north-

Left: *Notice remnants of packing crate hanging from steps with "A. H. S. Carls" written on it that was found in Magee Barn in 2001. A. H. S. stands for Alexander Hamilton Shipley, former owner of the barn.*

west corner. The site acquired the name Frazier's Station, after John Frazier opened his nearby mineral spring well and offered its waters to train passengers. The combination of water and train access opened the area for further development. When the Carlsbad Land and Water Company bought the land surrounding the rail lines and laid out a town, they changed the name of the station to Carlsbad. In 1907 the Santa Fe Railroad, trying to eliminate confusion between Carlsbad, California, and Carlsbad, New Mexico, shortened the station name to Carl. Citizen complaints forced the railway to reverse their decision rather quickly. The original depot for this station was an open shed that faced the rail lines. In 1888 the railway constructed the twenty-four-by-sixty-four-square-foot depot we currently enjoy. Ramps located on either side of the loading

Below: Commuter rail service, begun in the 1990s, once again connects Carlsbad by rail to the outside world.

Aerial looking northeast to original Carlsbad Airport at El Camino Real and Chestnut. (Courtesy Hayes-Marron Collection)

dock made it easier to move goods and produce from the train to the freight room or from farm wagons to the freight room for storage. For many years, the Carlsbad Train Station was the only way Carlsbad farmers could easily transport their crops to market.

Stewarts and Farr Stations, built south of the downtown station, handled freight and passenger service outside of the downtown Carlsbad area. Stewarts Station, constructed in 1884 close to present-day Palomar Airport Road, stored grain and goods for the W. W. Stewart and Company Shippers and Commission Merchants, who also had a warehouse in San Diego. A dirt road, known as Stewarts Road, ran east from the station towards San Marcos, north of and roughly parallel to present-day Palomar Airport Road. Bits and pieces of this road eventually became Palomar Airport Road. The San Diego Central Rail line, laid in 1887, connected Oceanside to Escondido. Before, inland rail service train passengers and freight came by stage or wagon to the coastal stations. The Hayes and Hicks Inland

Mail and Stage Company ran stages daily from the inland towns to the coastal rail lines. Stewarts Station was often the closest station for those traveling to the rail lines.

Farr Station, built near present-day Cannon Road, was another small station mainly used for loading agricultural produce. William Sherman Kelly used Farr Station for loading his hay, since it was the one closest to his ranch.

By 1960 the decline of ranching and farming in Carlsbad had contributed to a drop in freight service. The need for rail service to town was over, a casualty of better roads and housing developments. Through the instigation and persuasion of Chris Christiansen, the old Santa Fe Depot gained new life and purpose after the city of Carlsbad began administration of the site in 1963.

For almost three decades, trains passed through Carlsbad without stopping. In the 1990s the North County Transit District began a coastal commuter rail service. The Coaster runs on the same rail lines as Amtrak, linking all the coastal cities between Oceanside and San Diego. This service provides many of the same benefits to Carlsbad residents today as the original rail service provided in 1881. It reduces travel time to and from the city, facilitates the establishment of new businesses, and opens Carlsbad to new opportunities.

Aviation

Construction of Carlsbad's first airport occurred shortly after World War II. Constructed on Tom Borden's land on the eastern corner of El Camino Real and Chestnut, the sixteen-hundred-foot runway was a bulldozed dirt strip. A few of the men who left Carlsbad to fight in the war learned to fly during their military service. After the war was over, they were able to buy surplus planes called BTs or Basic Trainers from the Navy. Ralph Borden, Tom's son, was one of those wartime flyers. Noted for expertise with all things mechanical, he ran the small postwar airport. However, it was Cline Cantarini's instigation that fostered interest in flying for those Carlsbad boys who always wanted to learn how to fly. Affectionately known as an "airplane nut," Cantarini grew up in Carlsbad and flew in the Pacific during the war. Monte Yearly, Robert Farquhar, Louie Mitchell, Major Russell, and others contributed $50 each and bought a BT. Cantarini taught them to fly for the price of gas and oil. Cantarini inspired awe in those who knew him by flying a P-51, which he bought in Sacramento, to Carlsbad and landing on the dirt runway. This was a feat that amazed those who understood how difficult this was to accomplish. Adding to the low-tech features of the airport was the lack of automatic runway lighting. If a plane was due to arrive after dark, someone ran over to the airfield and plugged in the landing lights.

Many of the local flyers and businesses took steps in 1954 to bring a commercial airport to town. The Carroll Kelly property, southeast of Carlsbad, seemed a good site as it had plenty of vacant land around it for development of aviation-related businesses. One such business, located on Tyler Street, ran day and night shifts for production of Convair Interceptor parts.

Gerald McClellan, who first learned to fly at the old Chestnut airport and who was quoted as saying, "any reason in

Aerial looking northeast to original Carlsbad Airport on Borden land; old Highway 78 is visible in midsection of photo. (Courtesy Hayes-Marron Collection)

the world was a good reason to go flying," was instrumental in the early planning stages of developing the new commercial Palomar Airport. Groundbreaking ceremonies took place on June 24, 1958. Shortly after, in 1959, Palomar Airport opened with a thirty-seven-hundred-foot runway. Forty years later, in 1999, Palomar-McClellan, so named in 1981 to honor Gerald McClellan, was the fifth most active airport in the nation. Accommodating private and commercial planes that use a forty-six-hundred-foot airstrip, this airport processes 290,000 takeoffs and landings a year, compared to 250,000 at San Diego's Lindbergh Field. ❧

Carlsbad realtor Claude Fennel, on right, and pilot Ed Lines pose in front of biplane, circa 1928. (Courtesy San Diego Historical Society)

CHAPTER 13

Schools in Carlsbad

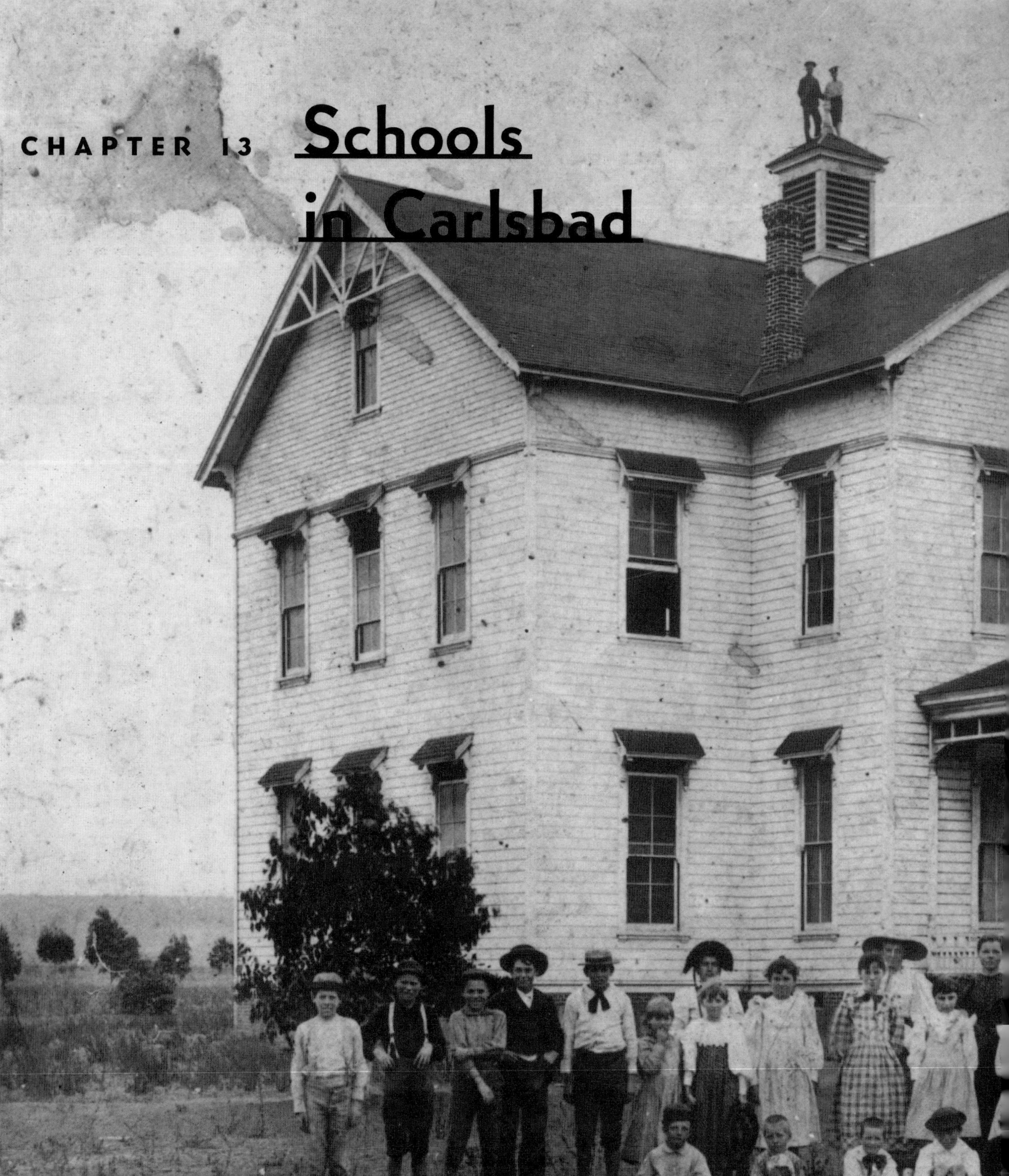

Trying to understand the Carlsbad School System is a challenge for anyone new to town. Where else does one find a single city with four separate public school districts? To make any sense of this School System labyrinth, one needs to understand the connection between Carlsbad's growth and development as a community and the growth of the School System.

Today the City of Carlsbad's geographical boundaries are larger than the original seven square miles incorporated in 1952 or even the Rancho Agua Hedionda land grant. In 1872, when a substantial amount of present-day Carlsbad was homestead land, families who settled and farmed in the area needed a school for their children. Hope School, built in 1872 close to the site of the current La Costa Resort, answered the schooling needs of the homesteaders. While this area did not become a part of Carlsbad until one hundred years later in 1972, it is the first school built in present-day Carlsbad.

The first school was built in downtown Carlsbad on Pine Street, circa 1894. It was simply known as the "Carlsbad School."

Three homestead families, the Adams, Feelers, and Kellys, helped construct the one-room dirt-floor school for the education of their children. Hope School opened with twenty-five students. The oldest was twenty-one years of age and all twenty-five students came from just the three previously mentioned families. The teaching staff frequently changed and was not well trained. Reevaluation of student academic placement and ability occurred after each teacher change. John Lincoln Kelly, a Hope School alumnus, stated, "Many of the teachers would have been better suited as farm laborers than teachers" (Life on a San Diego County Ranch," Kelly). Records show that Hope School operated until the 1890s.

In 1886, the Carlsbad Land and Water Company in a real estate venture developed land northwest of Rancho Agua Hedionda. Capitalizing on the recent discovery of water and the boom in Southern California real estate, the company began laying out roads and subdividing land into building plots that they then sold to families moving into the area. Families in town meant children in the area and a small one-room building became their schoolhouse. The school, with teacher Dr. Amick, became overcrowded within a very short time. Students and

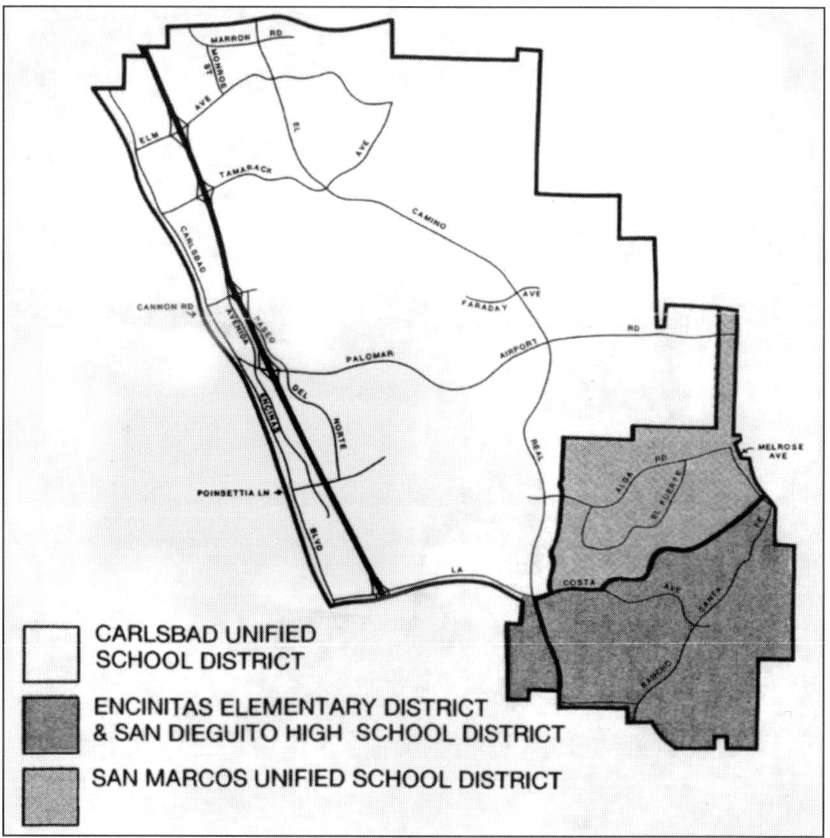

School District Boundaries, 2002.

teacher moved to the larger Schuttuck Building on Second and Elm. After this structure burned down, the residents of the town constructed a third building specifically designed as a school. It was unfortunate that just around the time construction began on this four-room two-story schoolhouse, a real estate downturn occurred, families moved away, students left and Carlsbad barely survived. Miss Hattie Reece, who taught at the newly constructed Carlsbad School, recalled her class size enrollment at thirty-six students in 1894, which dropped to an average of five or six after 1896.

Top: In 1987 the last stand of eucalyptus trees at the original Calavera School site were removed when Calavera Park was constructed. The trees were planted by schoolchildren around 1896.

Bottom: The remains of a cistern at Calavera School site, ten feet deep and twelve feet in diameter, was removed in 1987 when Calavera Park was constructed.

The few folks that remained in Carlsbad were ranch families, like the Marrons, who arrived in the area as early as 1840. The Marrons, Bordens, and Kellys decided that the Carlsbad School located on Pine Street in the downtown area was too far and inconvenient for their children to attend. So in 1896 they followed their parents' example and provided a school for their children, the Calavera School. The Kelly and Borden children, who attended the Hope School in 1872, built the Calavera School. The Calavera School building was actually an abandoned silkworm cocoonery that the families moved from the defunct Minneapolis Beach Colony near Cannon Road over to the Calavera site using horsepower on unpaved ranch roads.

Hope and Calavera Schools ran as long as there were ranch families that needed a school close to their homes. Once the

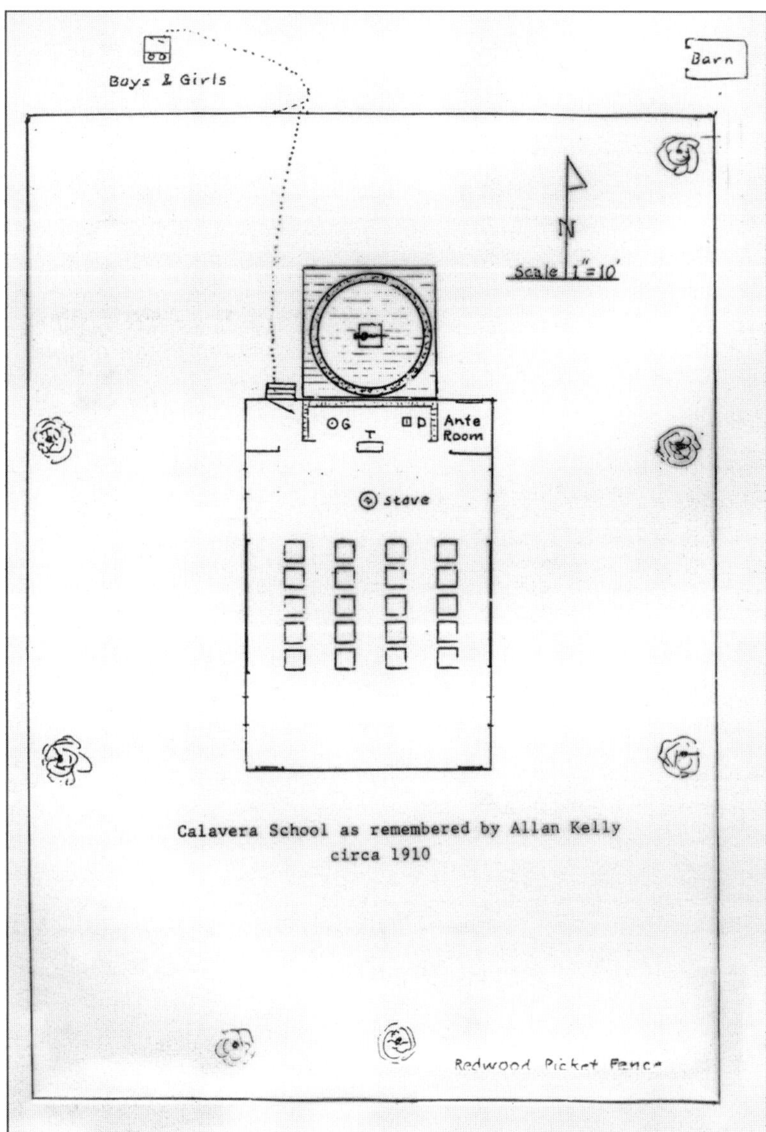

Calavera School as remembered by Allan Kelly circa 1910

children no longer needed the schools because they had left Carlsbad to attend secondary education elsewhere or because they had reached adulthood, the schools closed. When Calavera School ceased operation in 1919, it sent all of its furniture and school equipment to the Carlsbad School on Pine Street.

The arrival of the South Coast Land Company gave the Carlsbad School and town a new lease on life in the early 1900s. They guaranteed a potable water supply from their wells along the San Luis Rey River. Farmers started arriving in town bringing their families and increasing school enrollments.

In 1924 a larger school was built on Pine Street to accommodate all the new students. During one summer, demolition occurred on the old two-story schoolhouse and a more modern larger structure was completed after approval of a $16,000 construction bond. As the only public elementary school in Carlsbad, the Carlsbad School added to this building between 1924 and after World War II. It was not until other elementary schools were constructed in Carlsbad that the name *Carlsbad School* changed to *Pine School* in the 1940s. Through the combined efforts and guidance of School Board Trustee Cal Young and Principal and Superintendent Walter Glines, the groundwork for community support for schools during the Depression and World War II was laid. These two men, Young and Glines, made sure that the school system gave back to the community whenever possible. They made the school auditorium available for town meetings and as a civilian defense repository during World War II. The community repaid their efforts by approving five separate school bonds, one after another, immediately after the war.

The postwar baby boom that affected the entire country hit Carlsbad with a vengeance. Trying to keep pace with the population explosion, the Carlsbad Union School Board projected the number of future schools and classrooms needed. Their projections were obsolete before completion of a school's construction. Long gone were the days when accommodating an increase in student population could be solved by simply moving to a larger building or even adding a few extra classrooms to an existing school. Double sessions, the stopgap solution for overcrowding became the trend while waiting for the newest elementary school to be built. Trying to keep abreast of the population growth, construction of three elementary schools, Jefferson, Magnolia, and Buena Vista, and one high school, Carlsbad High, occurred between 1952 and 1962. The sheer number of teenagers in Carlsbad had finally warranted building the first high school in the town's history. Before the construction of Carlsbad High School, a student who graduated from eighth grade in the Carlsbad Union School District went to the combined Oceanside Carlsbad High founded in 1908, or left North County for schools in San Diego or Los Angeles.

The California State Board of Education had a minimum ten-thousand-population requirement for establishment of a school district. An increase in Carlsbad's student population meant the city was finally able to meet the requirement that would permit the unifying of grades K–12 in one school district. The California State Board of Education set stringent requirements for district formation because they felt it was easier to monitor and control a few megadistricts rather than many smaller ones. The State Board pushed for one megadistrict to govern a combined Carlsbad Union and Oceanside Union Elementary Schools and Oceanside Carlsbad Union High School. The California State Board of Education thought that schools in megadistricts operated more economically by wasting less and using tax money better, because it averaged upper and lower tax base money for the benefit of all within an area. Elections were held three times to unify all the school districts in Oceanside and Carlsbad and three times the issue was defeated.

Carlsbad residents rejected the idea of a combined Oceanside Carlsbad megadistrict because they believed the absolute number of students in a megadistrict would cause a loss of community identity. They also believed that Carlsbad and Oceanside had different educational philosophies. Finally, in 1970, Carlsbad was able to persuade the California State Board of Education to hold one more school district election. Dr. Ron Packard, president of the Carlsbad Union School District was able to prove to the State Board of Education that a unified Carlsbad School District would meet the Board's ten-thousand-student requirement for district formation. He used a projected student growth population analysis based on continued rapid development in the city. The Board of Education set an election date to decide if formation of a Carlsbad School District would occur. Overwhelmingly, in a six to one vote on June 3, 1970, Proposition T passed and Carlsbad Unified School District became a reality.

Two years later, in 1972, the neighborhood of La Costa requested annexation to Carlsbad. Until this time, as a mostly undeveloped area, La Costa had few full-time residents. Those that did live there all year who sent their children to public school, did so mainly in Carlsbad. Logically, one would think that the La Costa students would automatically be included in the Carlsbad Unified School District. But before this decision could be reached, the loss of potential tax money on surrounding communities needed to be considered. School districts in San Dieguito, Encinitas, and San Marcos were faced with the loss of projected student populations. Additionally a group of La Costa residents objected to sending their children eight miles north to the closest Carlsbad school. One unnamed San Diego County official admitted the issue was a political decision, not necessarily best for La Costa. In the end, each of the four school districts won a piece of the La Costa pie.

Carlsbad, Encinitas, San Marcos, and San Dieguito School Districts have all constructed new schools in the La Costa neighborhood to keep pace with the rapid rise in student population as the area developed. The "sense of community identity" vital to Carlsbad voters in 1970 is curiously lacking in today's multiple school district boundaries, since more and more of Carlsbad children attend school outside of the Carlsbad Unified School District.

Carlsbad High School

In 1955, Carlsbad and Oceanside voters approved a $1.26-million construction bond that funded the building of Carlsbad's first public high school. The Carlsbad High School cornerstone laid in September 1957 included a time capsule box containing a copy of a 1957 *Carlsbad Journal*, the first edition of the Carlsbad High

School newspaper, a student handbook, and 1957-minted coins.

Carlsbad High students began the 1957–58 academic year by commuting to Oceanside. They attended class in Oceanside High since construction of Carlsbad High was unfinished. Carlsbad students had always traveled to Oceanside to attend high school. For the first time ever, Carlsbad and Oceanside students attended separate classes. Each school ran their own class schedule within Oceanside High School and had separate student governments, athletic programs, and school newspapers.

On February 17, 1958, Carlsbad High students left Oceanside High amidst grand fanfare. A parade of buses and cars wove their way from Oceanside to the Carlsbad border, led by the Oceanside Police. At the Carlsbad border, the Carlsbad Police assumed parade leadership, touring the students past the

During the Depression the Woman's Club building was moved to Pine School for use as an auditorium.

Army and Navy Academy. The entire Cadet student population stood at attention while their band played a "Welcome Home" song for Carlsbad High Students. As the parade continued through the decorated downtown, many business owners and residents lined the streets cheering the newly arrived high school students. Carlsbad Mayor Manuel Castorena presented Carlsbad High Principal Alfred La Fleur with the key to the city.

This began the many "firsts" associated with Carlsbad High: The first public high school in Carlsbad and the "first" gymnasium. The Class of 1961 was the "first" class to attend CHS for their entire four years. Coach Swede Kracmar was the "first" CHS football coach to lead his team to three CIF small school championships (in 1961,1962 and 1965). The "first" Homecoming king was in 1976 (earlier there were only Homecoming queens). It was also the year that the "first" community swimming pool, one shared by the high school and the city, was constructed. The year 1982 saw the construction of Carlsbad's "first" Cultural Arts Center, located on the CHS campus. The high school newspaper, the *Lancer Express*, for the "first" time won four national honors in 1998–99 and the year 2000 was the "first" time the CHS surf team won all four divisions of CISF, an unprecedented event for any one high school team.

Carlsbad/Pine School

The Carlsbad School, which opened in 1894, was a two-story wooden structure built on Pine Street, an area then considered the outskirts of town. As the only school in the newly established town, children either attended the Carlsbad School or were sent to San Diego or Los Angeles for their education.

Miss Hattie Reece, an Oceanside resident, became the first teacher at the newly constructed Carlsbad School. Students fondly remembered her impact and devotion. After her mar-

Carlsbad School pediment.

riage to Alfred Schutte she remained in town raising her family and working as a social reporter for various local newspapers.

In 1924 a larger school replaced the old two-story schoolhouse. Demolition of the 1896 building occurred during the summer and it was replaced with a more modern concrete building by fall. Throughout the years under the administration and guidance of several principals and School District superintendents, such as Blanche Crane and Walter Glines, additions were made that enhanced the Carlsbad School.

In 1928, the Boy Scouts placed a log cabin on the school grounds. During the Depression in the 1930s, a Works Progress Administration project earthquake-proofed the grammar school and built a cement ring that circled the outside lunch area. It was later used as a recreational roller rink. The Women's Club, facing financial hardships during this time, sold their clubhouse across the street to the school for use as an auditorium. It was later converted into the school cafeteria.

Walter Glines, whose career as superintendent of Carlsbad Schools spanned the years 1941 to 1958, was instrumental in ending segregation of the English- and Spanish-speaking students in school.

In 1946, voters approved five school bonds for the construction of additional elementary schools in Carlsbad. It was at this time that the school's name was changed from Carlsbad School to Pine School. An agreement reached in 1988 between the city of Carlsbad and the Carlsbad Unified School District allowed construction of a shared building housing a Senior Center and School District Administration Office on the grounds of the original Carlsbad/Pine School. The only historical remnant from this site is a cracked pediment inscribed "CARLSBAD SCHOOL," located over the main entrance to the Carlsbad Unified School District offices.

Valley Junior High

As Carlsbad's student population continued to rise throughout the 1950s, the Carlsbad Unified School District recognized the need for a separate Junior High School. With the construction of the very first school in town in 1894, Carlsbad had always housed students in kindergarten through eighth grade in Carlsbad/Pine School. In 1955, the Carlsbad Unified School District bought land on the corner of Valley and Magnolia for the future construction of a separate Junior High School.

Jefferson Elementary School was the first school built in Carlsbad after World War II.

After years of planning, the School Board approved an architectural design for the future school. The design facilitated the construction and placement of new buildings on the campus, as dictated by future student growth. After 1966, seventh and eighth grade students no longer attended Pine School, instead they matriculated at Valley Junior High. One year after opening its doors, the School Board approved expansion of the newly constructed Valley Junior High School in a bid to stem student overcrowding.

Jefferson School

Built in 1952, Jefferson was the second school built in the Carlsbad Unified School District.

Magnolia Elementary

Magnolia Elementary school was Carlsbad's third elementary school and opened in March of 1957. By constructing this school the School Board hoped to eliminate the overcrowding of Carlsbad elementary schools. The Carlsbad Public Works Department moved a thirty-foot-high magnolia tree to Magnolia School from Roosevelt Street. The tree was planted in memory of Carlsbad Union School Board Member Billy C. Fry.

Kelly School

Kelly School, built in 1977, was named in recognition of the Kelly family, inheritors of the Rancho Agua Hedionda land grant.

Calavera School

Calavera School, located at the site of the present-day Calavera Park, was built originally as a silkworm cocoonery. Moved to the site, the building was made of lath and plaster with a redwood exterior and tongue-and-groove floor. After the school closed in 1920, a country dance hall occupied the building and site. In 1986, a ten-foot wide by twelve-foot deep cistern used to collect rainwater, and a line of eucalyptus trees planted by the first class of students in 1896 were still on the grounds when park construction began.

School assembly at Magnolia Elementary, circa 1990s, views a hot-air balloon.

CHAPTER 14 Parks in Carlsbad

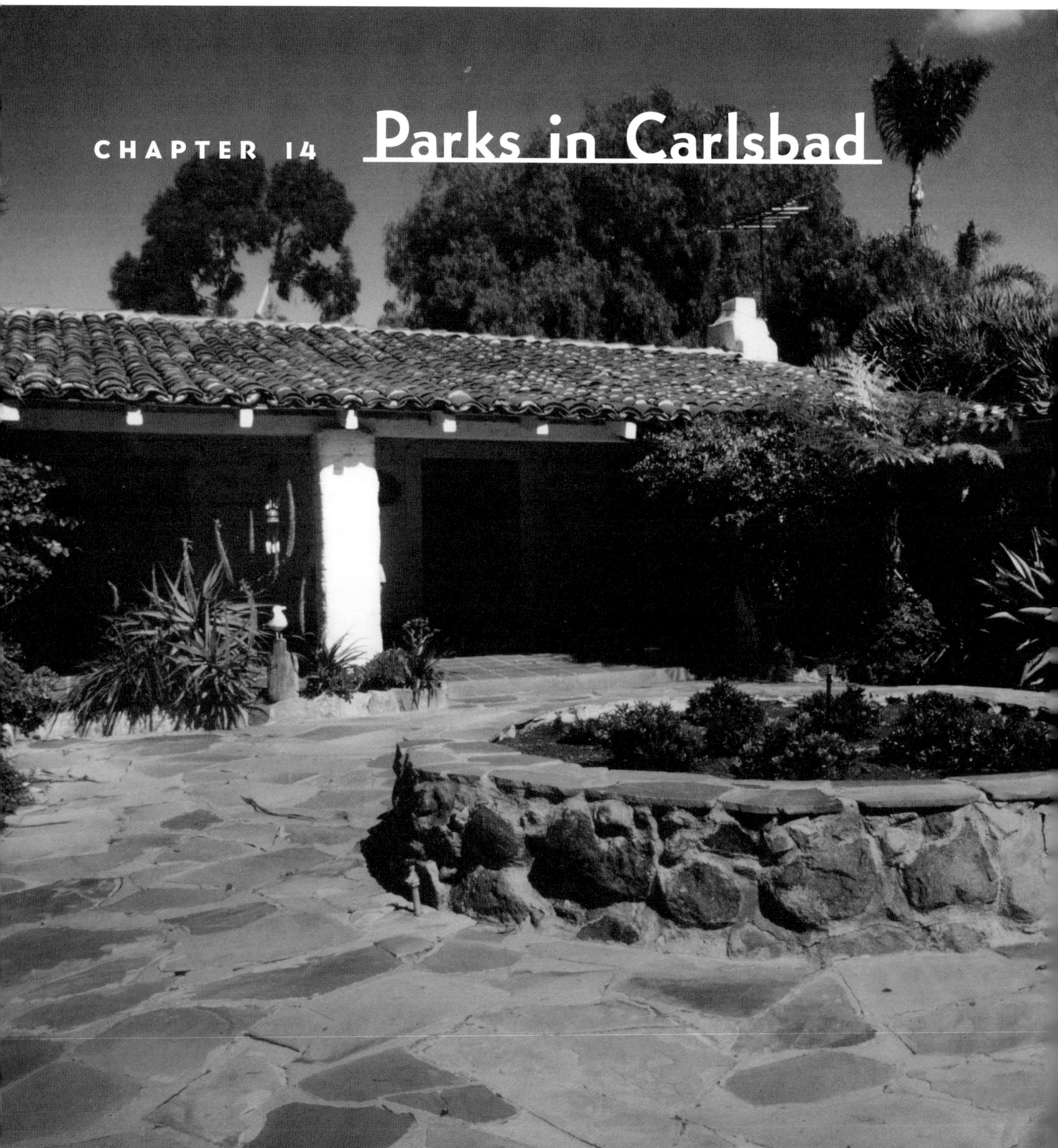

Carlsbad's Parks and Recreation Department began in 1954 with the acquisition of its first park, Holiday Park, and the appointment of its first employee, Superintendent Nelson Westree. In the years immediately after incorporation, when the city treasury was limited, new departments were gradually added into the city government budget as the funds became available. Prior to the establishment of the Parks and Recreation Department, a volunteer group that served a similar function was called the Park, Beach, and Recreational Commission. Many of the early city employees were volunteers who worked part time for the city while continuing in other occupations. As park superintendent, Mr. Westree worked part time while continuing as groundsperson for the Carlsbad Hotel, and tending to his own macadamia nut groves. In 1948, when the Westree family arrived in Carlsbad, they promptly began volunteering in their new neighborhood. When asked in a 1969 interview why they volunteered, Mrs. Westree responded, "I simply believe that you have to figure your own 'good' things in life . . . maybe money isn't as important as we think it is . . . maybe happiness and satisfaction in the job are equally important." When asked thirty years later if she still felt the same way about volunteering, Mrs. Westree added, "We owe something to life, we shouldn't take up space, we should make a contribution to where we are living."

Home of Leo Carrillo at Carrillo Ranch or the Flying LC.

Spring Holiday Pet Show participants.

Gradually the Carlsbad Parks and Recreation Department grew from a mostly volunteer organization with one part-time employee and one park site, to an organization that today includes a variety of parks, community centers, sports programs, and enrichment classes. Many of the land additions to the park system have interesting and unique stories behind their acquisition.

In 1954 the San Diego County Department of Roads sold to the city of Carlsbad, for $300, three acres of county-owned land that the department used as a road equipment storage yard. After the purchase, civic debate arose on what would be the best use of the land. Some residents suggested reselling the property and putting the money into the city treasury, others wanted to construct a library, and still others wanted a park. Mr. Westree conducted a random phone survey and presented the results to the City Council. The land that was bordered by I-5, Basswood, Eureka, and Chestnut finally became the genesis of the Carlsbad Park System and was named Holiday Park, in honor of the annual Spring Holiday Event begun in 1951 by the Carlsbad Rotary.

Every participant went home a winner from the Spring Holiday Pet Show.

Rotary Park

Rotary Park, located on Grand and Washington, is another city acquisition with an interesting origin that also points to the significance and importance of the resident volunteer spirit that benefited the community. By 1960 trains were no longer stopping in Carlsbad for freight or passenger service. The 1888 Santa Fe Station was deteriorating. B. M. (Chris) Christiansen and his wife Kay shared a keen interest in history. It was the Christiansens' shared dream to reopen the Carlsbad Mineral Spring Well, and with this in mind they purchased the property on which the original mineral wells were located. Chris and Kay became founding members of the Carlsbad Historical Society. While researching primary historical documentation relating to the Mineral Well, it also enabled them to gather information relating to early Carlsbad history. Considering Chris's civic involvement and his interest in local history it was not surprising that he expressed concern in 1960 over the vacant Santa Fe Train Depot that was becoming a downtown eyesore. With his typical energy, Mr. Christiansen, wearing his president of the Carlsbad Rotary hat, contacted the president of the Santa Fe Railroad, who also happened to be president of Rotary International. Christiansen was able to convince him that it would be in everyone's best interest to let the community have use of the historic building as well as a few acres of land. The site was designated as Rotary Park and through volunteer efforts the old Depot was cleaned up as well as the land around it.

Maxton Brown Bird Sanctuary

In 1965, a small three-acre park was dedicated as Lt. Maxton Brown Jr. Bird Sanctuary on Laguna Drive overlooking the Buena Vista Lagoon. Maxton Brown Jr. was lost while flying over North Africa during World War II. Prior to the war he spent many hours at the lagoon sighting and recording over 150 species of birds. In consideration of his dedication to the Buena Vista Lagoon and to its inhabitants, the bird sanctuary carries his name.

Magee Park

Magee Park was acquired by the city in 1974 when Florence Shipley Magee passed away, willing her home and the property around it to the city of Carlsbad for a historic and recreational park. This bountiful donation was the partial answer to a serious dilemma facing the city. In 1971 a report to the mayor and City Council pointed out that because the city lacked an adequate industrial tax base it was not in a financial position to acquire or develop new parks.

In 1972, the chairperson of the Parks and Recreation Commission, Betty Wollrich, proposed a $1-million bond election for purchase and development of neighborhood parkland. This bond election was in direct response to a city questionnaire that stated 90 percent of Carlsbad residents wanted more parks. In 1972 Carlsbad owned just thirteen acres of parkland. The hope was that bond approval would allow the city to increase that to a total of forty park acres.

SPRING HOLIDAY EVENT

The Spring Holiday Event was conceived as a way to highlight the achievements of Carlsbad's principal volunteer organizations. An annual week-long event, it offered an opportunity to participate to everyone in the community. Once the land was acquired and dedicated as Holiday Park, the park became a venue for one of the activities: a community cookout. Other venues were staged throughout town to accommodate the various Spring Holiday events. The activities included operettas performed at the Army and Navy Academy Auditorium, Carnival rides at Saint Patrick's Church, Zany Hat Breakfast held at the Carlsbad Woman's Club, downtown parades, a pet show at the Union Church, and water-skiing exhibitions at Agua Hedionda Lagoon. The entire Spring Holiday Event culminated with a huge dinner dance held at two sites, the Twin Inns and across the street at the Carlsbad Hotel. The week long Spring Holiday Event was staged each year through the 1950s and 60s and it truly was a community event, organized and enjoyed by all. It was only appropriate that the first community park should be named in honor of such a community holiday event.

A two-thirds majority vote was necessary for passage of the park acquisition bond. This bond would tax 11 cents on every accessed $100 of land valuation. Opponents to the bond issue expressed discontent with the tax assessment and suggested that other methods be exhausted before more taxes were levied. With a 54.6 percent approval of the park bond, it failed to gain the necessary number of votes and the city was forced to find other ways to add more land to their park system.

353413

STATE OF NEW YORK.

County of New York. City of New York.

BIRTH RETURN.

1. Name of Child (in full when possible.) Florence Shipley
2. Sex Female Color or Race, if other than the White, Date of Birth Nov. 15th 1882
3. Place of Birth (Street and Number) 61 Canal Street
4. Name of Father Alexander Shipley (If out of wedlock and name not given, write O. W.)
5. Full Name of Mother Julia Shipley
6. Maiden Name of Mother Julia Seamont
7. Birthplace (Country or State) of Mother City of New York Age 30
8. " " of Father New York Age 34 Occupation Artist
9. Number of Child of Mother (whether 1, 2, 3, &c.) First How many of them now living 1
10. Name and address of Medical Attendant or other Authorized person, in own handwriting Minnie Kruger 195 Forsyth Street
11. Date of this Return 23rd Nov. 1882

The Parks and Recreation Department made a list of what Carlsbad lacked and what was desired: more ball parks, elimination of lumpy school tennis courts, enlargement of the undersized soccer fields, more basketball courts, and at least one community swimming pool. With this list in mind the city needed to find ways to resolve and correct what was lacking in the park system.

A variety of solutions presented themselves. In 1979 the city and the school district entered into an agreement that would guarantee joint use of school facilities. This eventually led to the 1980s construction of a community pool on Carlsbad High School grounds. Additionally, a Park Dedication Ordinance was enacted that required developers to either give land or money for park acquisition and development.

When Florence Magee's will bequeathed her home and gardens to the City of Carlsbad for use within the park system in 1974, it was a most welcome and needed addition, since the city had none of the previously mentioned solutions. The land surrounding Mrs. Magee's home eventually provided a home for other displaced historical buildings, such as Heritage Hall, originally Saint Patrick's Catholic Church on Harding Street. Later the church was used as Carlsbad's first Police Department, City Hall, and Library. Without question Magee Park, with Mrs. Magee's home as a centerpiece, is one of Carlsbad's most unique and special parks, providing a glimpse of a more tranquil time.

Top: Florence Shipley was born in New York City in 1882.

Above: The Magee House and grounds were donated by Florence Shipley Magee for use as a city park.

Magee House and Its Inhabitants

Samuel Church Smith, one of the founding members of the Carlsbad Land and Water Company, originally constructed the house in 1886. It has retained much of its original charm, having housed only two families. The Smith family lived for a few short years in Carlsbad before moving to San Diego. It was left empty until 1896, when the Shipley family arrived looking for a healthier place in which to live. Florence, an only child, was fourteen years old on her arrival with her parents, Alexander and Julia. Originally from New York, the family had more recently lived in Napa, California, after returning from New Zealand, where Mr. Shipley served as vice consul for the U.S. government. Quite wealthy with financial investments throughout California and the United States, well educated and traveled, the family had a difficult adjustment to small-town Carlsbad. However, Mr. Shipley suffered from a variety of ailments that caused considerable strain and upheaval on the family. Carlsbad, with its yearlong springlike climate, seemed ideal for Alexander's health.

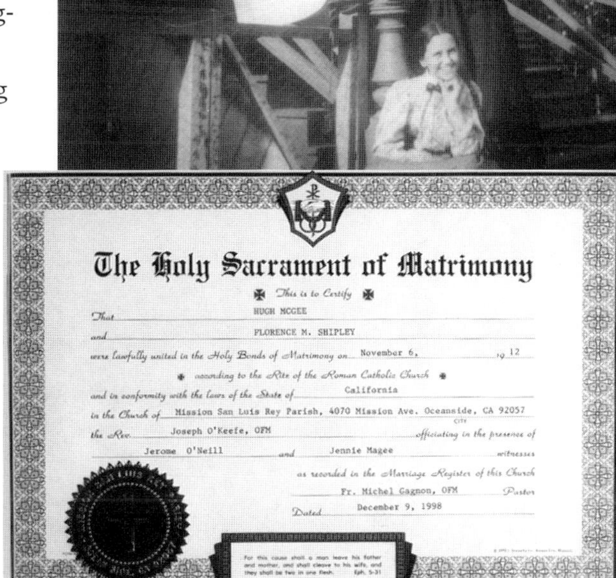

The Holy Sacrament of Matrimony

This is to Certify

That HUGH MCGEE

and FLORENCE M. SHIPLEY

were lawfully united in the Holy Bonds of Matrimony on November 6, 19 12

according to the Rite of the Roman Catholic Church

and in conformity with the laws of the State of California

in the Church of Mission San Luis Rey Parish, 4070 Mission Ave. Oceanside, CA 92057

the Rev. Joseph O'Keefe, OFM officiating in the presence of

Jerome O'Neill and Jennie Magee witnesses

as recorded in the Marriage Register of this Church

Fr. Michel Gagnon, OFM Pastor

Dated December 9, 1998

For this cause shall a man leave his father and mother, and shall cleave to his wife, and they shall be two in one flesh. Eph. 5-31

Top: Florence Shipley, sitting on the banister at left, is surrounded by school friends in San Diego.

Above: Florence Shipley married Hugh Magee at Mission San Luis Rey on November 6, 1912.

Florence was educated at Our Lady of Peace Academy, a Catholic boarding school in San Diego. Upon her graduation in 1902, Florence was given an opportunity to do a bit of traveling.

However, the 1906 San Francisco earthquake also had a profound impact on the Shipley family finances. This setback, plus her father's failing health, forced Florence to accept considerable responsibility for handling much of the family's business affairs. Considering that this took place in a time when women in this country

In this group, Florence and Hugh Magee are third and fourth from the left.

Top: These members of the Arboretum and Coastal Rose Groups are volunteer gardeners at Magee Park. (Caswell Collection)

Above: Magee Garden in bloom.

were still not allowed to vote, it points to the great respect that Mr. Shipley showed for his daughter's intellectual abilities.

In 1912, after Florence married Hugh Magee, she left Carlsbad for over twenty-nine years, living at Condor's Nest, the Magee family ranch near Pala. Florence was able to visit her parents often, considering the difficulty of travel over unpaved roads, and the difficulty of leaving a working ranch. A close relationship with her parents was maintained through her almost daily correspondence.

In 1941, after Hugh's death, the childless Florence returned to Carlsbad and lived with her widowed mother. After her mother's death in 1943, Florence remained alone in her family home for the next thirty years with just her pet cats as companions. So numerous and well known were her pets, that in 1985, after her death, their descendants were still living around the park. Irma Algover, who lived nearby, often fed the semiwild cats. When asked why she did this, Ms. Algover said that when she looked at their hungry eyes, she remembered herself and other Hungarian refugees who fled Europe during World War II. The cats had the same look.

After the city acquired the Magee home, some renovations were required to bring the house into compliance with modern safety standards. However, for the most part the original structure remains. Today, two volunteer gardening groups, the Carlsbad Arboretum Foundation and Coastal Rose Society, maintain the gardens that surround the home. Various planting themes that dominate the flower beds: plants native to Southern California, those grown commercially in Carlsbad, and of course old garden roses as well as modern teas, provide an interesting history lesson to those who visit.

Carrillo Ranch

In the years immediately after acquisition of Magee Park, four additional sites in Carlsbad with unique historical connections were incorporated into the Carlsbad Parks and Recreation Department. In 1977, through a provision of the Quimby Act, Carlsbad received ownership of 10.5 acres of the Carrillo Ranch, the former weekend home of Hollywood star Leo Carrillo. The Quimby Act is a California state provision in which a developer may give land instead of fees to a city or county so that the city or county are able to acquire land for future parks. This developer-donated land or fees are specifically earmarked for park acquisitions. The intent of the Quimby Act is to guarantee sufficient parkland for new residential communities. The original developers of Rancho Carrillo dedicated the 10.5 acres to the city of Carlsbad twenty years before the first house was built. Park plans drawn by the city were intended to use the special features at Carrillo Ranch to highlight the ambiance of the old California-style ranch, and to create an environment applicable for general public use. In 2001 the park was still unavailable for public use due to lack of funding for renovation and restoration as well as conversion from a working ranch to an interpretive park. Currently, the City of Carlsbad is in the process of restoring and seismic retrofitting all existing buildings as funds become available. Plans call for the opening of Carrillo Ranch in the near future.

Before 1982, acquisition of parks in the City of Carlsbad was a haphazard and opportunistic affair. In 1982, the Carlsbad General Plan added a Parks and Recreation Element that incorporated a long-range strategy for location of parks throughout the city. In spite of the city's plans, the citizens of Carlsbad had a few ideas of their own.

Hosp Grove

One of the changes to the Parks and Recreation overall park plan was the addition of Hosp Grove. Hosp Grove's existence began in 1908 when forty-five acres of land were planted with over forty thousand eucalyptus trees overlooking Buena Vista Lagoon. Nurseryman F. P. Hosp secured investment funds from Messrs. Martin, McGee, and Whitaker. They collectively formed the Hosp Eucalyptus Corporation. The original focus of the corporation was to plant 219 acres

In the mid-1980s, after the sale of the Twin Inns Restaurant, two of the restaurant's famous plaster chickens were moved next door to Rotary Park. Less than forty-eight hours later, the chickens were stolen. In December of 1989 one plaster chicken was found abandoned in an apartment house dumpster. Currently the last of the Twin Inns' chickens can be viewed at the Carlsbad Historical Society Museum at Magee Park.

with fast-growing, drought-tolerant trees that could be harvested for use as railroad ties. The plans came to naught when they discovered that the eucalyptus trees were inadequate for this purpose. Over the years Hosp Grove shrank as parcels of land were sold off for housing developments.

Hosp Grove held a special place in many local hearts as a childhood playground, where as kids they camped out or rode horses. After construction of the Plaza Camino Real Mall in the late 1960s and widening of Highway 78, the eucalyptus trees in Hosp Grove became the tranquil guardians of Carlsbad's northern border. In 1986, the remaining eucalyptus-filled acres went on the market for $6.5 million. Fearing commercial development of this last bit of open space in the northern end of town, a citizen-initiated proposition was placed on the ballot. If passed, it would require the city to purchase a total of fifty-three acres of land. After two election attempts the proposition passed, thus authorizing the city of Carlsbad to pay the asking price of $6.5 million dollars.

Top: Hosp Grove, circa 1906.

Above and right: Hosp Grove, circa 2001.

The city argued it could not afford the Hosp Grove asking price. The Sustain Hosp Grove Committee agreed with the city government's argument and opposed purchase of the fifty-three acres. Sponsored by many of Carlsbad's former mayors, the Sustain Hosp Grove group proposed an alternative solution that would honor citizens' wishes and at the same time allow the city to afford the purchase. Their proposal required the city to lease some of the Hosp Grove acres for commercial development, thus generating the funds needed to purchase the entire fifty-three acres.

A second group, Save Our Open Space, rejected the Sustain Hosp Grove's proposal. Offering a proposal of their own, one that would thwart the Sustain Hosp Grove pro-

posal, it would require a two-thirds vote for any rezoning of designated open space land. Many City Council meetings discussed possible ways to honor the election results and buy Hosp Grove. A solution was reached, when the city "borrowed" money from itself, in order to close the deal. What the city did was use money designated for another use to finalize the purchase. This gave the city breathing room it needed to make the purchase, secure a more permanent way to pay for the land, and rework the future city budget to include this new expense.

Today, Hosp Grove, owned by the city of Carlsbad, provides a natural environment for Carlsbad's citizens by retaining a eucalyptus-filled oasis in the midst of urban development.

Below: This enclosure at Stagecoach Park, 2001, protects the remains of the Ybarras home/stagecoach stop.

Bottom: Close-ups of the remains of the Ybarras home/stagecoach stop before and (bottom) after construction of Stagecoach Park.

Stagecoach and Calavera Parks

In the late 1980s, Carlsbad constructed two parks, Stagecoach and Calavera, on sites that had documented historical backgrounds. Each shared the same overall park design that included large recreation centers, baseball fields, and tennis and basketball courts. However, treatment of the historical sites was totally different. At Stagecoach Park, some conservation of the original historical structure remains, while at Calavera every aspect of its historical significance was removed.

Stagecoach Park occupies a small portion of the former Las Encinitas Rancho, a Mexican land grant given to Don Andres Ybarra in 1842. *Las Encinitas*, which translates into "Little Live Oaks," passed through many hands. In 1860, subsequent owners Joseph S. Mannassee and Marcus Schiller converted Don Ybarra's adobe home into a stagecoach stop. The remnants of this adobe structure can still be found on the grounds of Stagecoach Park beneath a roofed enclosure.

Calavera Park occupies the site of the former Calavera School, one of Carlsbad's earliest schools, begun in 1897. At the time of park construction in 1987, the land still retained some of the original features. A cistern used for

water collection and a grove of trees planted by the first group of students in 1897 was still on the property. None of the existing features were retained, protected, or included into the new park design.

Special Niche Parks

During the 1990s, the Parks Department planned and developed a variety of parks throughout Carlsbad according to the Carlsbad General Plan Park Element. A small Art Park was constructed in 1991 on Carlsbad Boulevard and Ocean Street. As part of the overall city streetscape improvement project, it was never part of the city Parks and Recreation Department. From the

Top: Before and after construction of Stagecoach Park.

Above, and inset: Construction of Stagecoach Park Community Center underway, 1987.

very beginning, this small triangular piece of land was embroiled in controversy. Before the park construction began, various agencies needed to approve different aspects of the plan. Delays occurred which pushed back construction. This delay caused financial hardship for businesses in the area. Some business owners claimed to have suffered as much as a 70 percent drop in revenue.

The next big issue faced was the design of the park itself. Community input was solicited and proposed designs of the new "art" park were made available to all residents. However, what the public viewed on display did not translate well once built. Huge wooden fences surrounded the site, within which a streamlined park centerpiece entitled *Split Pavilion*, designed by New York artist Andrea Blum, was constructed. When the unveiling occurred, *Split Pavilion* came to be known locally as "The Bars." Eight-foot-high galvanized metal bars framed the view of a reflection pool and the Pacific Ocean.

Construction of Calavera Community Park (above).

Critics complained that the resulting design was unlike anything they had viewed in the numerous public displays before construction. Cement, xeriscape plants, and metal provided a harsh vista for park visitors. Citizen protests convinced the city that something needed to be done to change the appearance of *Split Pavilion*. California laws protect artistic expression. Therefore, before changes occurred, an agreement had to be reached with the artist. On June 2, 1998, Carlsbad voters authorized the city to make a settlement with the artist. Known as the Carlsbad-Blum Settlement Agreement, changes desired by citizens were enacted over a period of years. Currently, the park itself has evolved into a site for expressionist art. A simple triangular strip of grassy

Continuing construction of Calavera Community Park.

Facing page: Ann (on the right) and Fletcher L'Heureux were advocates for Dog Park which opened 2001.

land facing the ocean provides a stage for street entertainers and spontaneous artistic displays.

In 1999 a Skate Park opened in response to complaints regarding the safety of pedestrians and skateboards coexisting on city streets. The city developed a series of cement shallow bowls, stairways, and handrails in a 15,000-square-foot open-air facility adjacent to the safety center.

Carlsbad's first Dog Park, which opened in September of 2001 off of Carlsbad Village Drive east of El Camino Real, is another example of citizen-generated changes in the overall park plan. The City of Carlsbad has an ordinance that restricts dogs on city parkland or beaches. In 1996, Ann L'Heureux asked the city to consider constructing a fenced park area for dogs, similar to those of other Southern California cities, a place where dog owners could allow their pets off leash. Finally, five years after the initial request, a 13,200-square-foot fenced park was dedicated for dog use.

Over a period of fifty years, the needs, interests, and finances of Carlsbad have grown. One can chart the progress of the city by looking at the evolution from a one-park town to a city where we can even provide special park space for our pets.

LOS KIOTES

Carrillo Ranch is just a small part of the former ten-thousand-acre Los Kiotes (Quiotes) Ranch, one of Carlsbad's oldest homesteads. In 1868, Matthew Kelly established a homestead south of Rancho Agua Hedionda land grant. The Kelly family retained title to this ranch until 1922, when Matthew's children sold off part of the land. In 1937, during the depth of the Great Depression, Leo Carrillo bought 840 acres of the land from a San Francisco syndicate and set about establishing a weekend retreat. Retaining part of the original Kelly adobe home, Carrillo was able to renovate and add to the structure, creating a replica of an old California-style rancho. His efforts to create a working ranch were completed with the addition of a barn, bunkhouse, as well as other ranch structures.

APPENDIX 1 — Carlsbad Time Line

1769 Spanish Soldiers in the Sacred Expedition name Agua Hedionda Lagoon

1798 Mission San Luis Rey founded

1821 Mexico gains independence from Spain

1833 Mission lands secularized

1842 Land grant given to Juan Maria Marron known as Rancho San Francisco

1844 Rancho San Francisco's name changes to Rancho Agua Hedionda

1853 Marron dies; wife and children mortgage land

1860 Rancho Agua Hedionda now owned by Francis Hinton

1868 Matthew Kelly establishes Los Kiotes homestead south of Rancho Agua Hedionda

1870 Hinton's death leaves Robert Kelly as sole owner of Rancho Agua Hedionda

1872 Hope School District formed

1880 Rail line runs along coastline

1880 Thomas and Alfred Metcalf and Jacob Gruendike buy land around Batiquitos Lagoon

1881 John Frazier settles by rail line

1883 Frazier drills wells; discovers artesian and mineral water

1886 Carlsbad Land and Water Company formed

1887 Land along rail line named Carlsbad; real estate boom begins

1887 Metcalf and Gruendike form La Costa Town and Land Company

1890 Robert Kelly's death leaves Rancho Agua Hedionda to his brother Matthew's nine children

1890 General land bust; town stops growing

1896 Shipley family moves to town

1914 South Coast Land Company finalizes purchase of defunct Carlsbad Land and Water Company Land holdings

1914 Carlsbad turns to farming

1916 Sam Thompson arrives in town, plants first avocados

1919 Carlsbad Mutual Water Company formed

1919 Kentners buy Twin Inns Restaurant

1922 Flower industry begins

1923 Wesleyan Methodist Mission begins

1927 Completion of new Coast Highway diverts traffic from State Street

1929 Carlsbad Sanitation District formed

1930 Carlsbad Mineral Springs Hotel opens

1933 Carlsbad State Beach Park established

1936 Army Navy Academy moves to Carlsbad

1937 Leo Carrillo buys 1,609 acres of former Los Kiotes homestead

1941 Branch of Church of Jesus Christ of Latter Day Saints formed in Carlsbad

1942 United States Marine Corps moves to Rancho Santa Margarita which becomes Camp Pendleton

1943 Saint Patrick's becomes a parish

1950 Downtown street names changed from First through Fifth to State, Roosevelt, Madison, Jefferson, and Harding

1952 Carlsbad incorporates

1953 Freeway opens

1954 Parks and Recreation Department formed

1954 San Diego Gas and Electric opens Encina Power Plant

1954 Municipal Water Company formed

1956 Carlsbad establishes its own library system

1958 Carlsbad High School opens

1959 Palomar Airport opens

1960 First woman mayor, Jane Sonneman

1964	First buildings developed in La Costa
1966	Valley Junior High opens
1967	Mayor is directly elected for first time; Elm Street Library built and opened
1968	City Hall opened
1969	Plaza Camino Real Mall opens
1971	Carlsbad Unified School District formed
1972	La Costa annexes to Carlsbad
1977	Cultural Arts Center construction approved by voters
1977	Car Country Carlsbad opens
1981	Carlsbad triathlon started, Marcario Canyon purchased by city
1984	Mural painted on Circle K Market
1991	Caring Residents open shelter in Carlsbad
1994	Groundbreaking for La Costa Canyon High School
1999	Legoland opens
2000	Museum of Making Music opens

APPENDIX II — Elected Officials

Mayors Elected to City Council Then Appointed to Office

C. D. McClellan
July 1952–April 1955

Raymond C. Ede
April 1955–April 1956

Manuel Castorena
April 1956–April 1958

D. E. Baird
April 1958–July 1958

Carl Lough
July 1958–October 1958

C. B. Ledgerwood
October 1958–April 1960

William La Roche
April 1961–April 1962

E. H. McPherson
April 1962–April 1963

William G. Guevara
April 1963–March 1964

H. E. Bierce Jr.
March 1964–April 1964

Carl Neiswender
April 1964–April 1965

William C. Atkinson
April 1965–April 1966

Election of Mayors by Electors—1966

William C. Atkinson
April 1966–January 1968

David Dunne
April 1968–March 1974

Robert C. Frazee
March 1974–March 1978

Ronald C. Packard
March 1978–June 1982

Mary Casler
June 1982–December 1986

Claude A. Lewis
December 1986–to expire November 2002

Council Members

C. D. McClellan
June 1952–April 1954

Lena Sutton
June 1952–September 1955

Raymond Ede
June 1952–April 1956
Manuel Castorena
June 1952–April 1958
George Grober
June 1952–April 1960
Lew Chase
July 1953–April 1954
R. R. Robinson
September 1955–April 1958
Robert Sutton
April 1954–April 1956
Claud R. Helton
April 1954–May 1959
Charles Ledgerwood
April 1956–April 1960
David Baird
April 1956–June 1958
Carl Lough
April 1958–October 1958
Jane Sonneman
April 1958–April 1962
Margaret Coats
October 1958–October 1959
Earl McPherson
May 1959–April 1964
William La Roche
October 1959–April 1962
Gonzalo (Bill) Guevara
April 1960–June 1964
H. E. Bierce
April 1960–April 1964
Jack Hughes
April 1962–April 1966
Carl Neiswender
April 1962–April 1970
William Atkinson
April 1964–April 1966
J. E. Jardine
April 1964–April 1972
David Dunne
July 1964–April 1968
Ralph Worthing
June 1966–April 1968
Glenn McComas
April 1968–February 1975
Joe Castro
April 1968–April 1972
Claude A. Lewis
April 1970–December 1986
Robert Frazee
April 1972–March 1974
Lewis Chase
April 1972–March 1976
Anthony Skotnicki
June 1974–April 1980
Mary Casler
February 1975–June 1982
Ronald Packard
March 1976–March 1978
Girard Anear
March 1978–November 1982
Ann Kulchin
April 1980–to expire November 2004
Richard Chick
June 1982–December 1986
Robert Prescott
November 1982–November 1984
Mark Pettine
November 1984–November 1990
John Mamaux
November 1986–November 1990
Eric Larson
March 1987–November 1992
Margaret Stanton
November 1990–November 1994
Julianne Nygaard
November 1990–to expire November 2002
Ramona Finnila
November 1992–to expire November 2004
Matt Hall
November 1994–to expire November 2002

BIBLIOGRAPHY

Articles

Baird, Robert. "The Army and Navy Academy."

Board, Clara. "The Kelly's, 1819–1944." 1975.

Kelly, John Lincoln. "Life on a San Diego County Ranch." 1918.

Lamb, Jay R. "A Brief History of the Batiquitos Lagoon Area." *Local History* 43 (1977).

Watterson, Virginia J. "Local Historical Adobe Buildings." *Local History* 43 (1977).

Books

Harmon, Jack. *History of Carlsbad*. Carlsbad: Friends of the Library, 1967.

Hart, William T. *History of State and County Parks in San Diego County*. Edited by Heilbron, Carl, H. *History of San Diego County*. San Diego: San Diego Press Club, 1936.

Howard-Jones, Marge. *Seekers of the Spring*. Carlsbad: Friends of the Library, 1982.

Orton, Charles Wesley. *Carlsbad, The Village by the Sea*. Encinitas: Heritage Publishing, 1994.

Correspondence

Clark, Warren E. Correspondence. Anaheim, Calif., 1981.

Ledgerwood, Charles. Correspondence. Carlsbad, Calif., 1977.

San Diego County Health Department. Correspondence. San Diego, Calif., 1937 and 1953.

Consultant Reports

Phelps, Byrl. *Report on the Need for a New Sewage Treatment Plant for Carlsbad, California*. San Diego, Calif., September 1953.

Environmental Impact Profiles. *Environmental Impact Report for the Planned Community of Carlsbad Palisades*. San Clemente, Calif., March 1973.

League of Women Voters. *Know Your City*. Carlsbad, Calif., 1982.

Government Documents

Annexation of La Costa a Preliminary Report. City of Carlsbad, September 21, 1971.

Carlsbad General Plan. City of Carlsbad, 1994.

Carlsbad Report 12, no. 3. City of Carlsbad, 1985.

City of Carlsbad Waterworks Revenue Bonds. City of Carlsbad, July 1958.

Evolution of a Small Craft Harbor Development. Carlsbad, Calif., 1973.

Final Recommended Spheres of Influence. San Diego Local Agency Formation Commission, February 17, 1978.

Natural Resources of Agua Hedionda Lagoon. California Department of Fish and Game, U.S. Wildlife Service, June 1976.

Specifications for the Construction of Disposal Works and Main Trunk Lines of a Sewerage System. Carlsbad Sanitary District, August 1929.

Interviews

Barnes, Esther and Larry. Interview by author. Carlsbad, July 2001.

Caron, Shelly. Interview by author. Carlsbad, October 2001.

Ferris, Robert. Interview by author. Carlsbad, April 2001.

Henley, John. Interview by author. Carlsbad, May 2001.

Howard-Jones, Marge. Interview by author. Carlsbad, May 2001.

Jandro, Afton and Al. Interview by author. Carlsbad, May 2001.

Kelly, Allan. Interview by author. Carlsbad, August 2001.

Kentner, Edward Jr. Interview by author. Carlsbad, June 2001.

Kubota, Jack. Interview by author. Carlsbad, April 2001.

Lee, Dee Kentner. Interview by author. Carlsbad, June 2001.

L'Heureux, Ann. Interview by author. Carlsbad, September 2001.

Metzger, Rudy. Interview by author. Carlsbad, April 2001.

Miller, Jackie Kentner. Interview by author. Carlsbad, June 2001.

Pace, Roy. Interview by Georgia Banks. Carlsbad, September 1972.

Westree, Ede. Interview by author. Carlsbad, August 2001.

Yearley, Monte. Interview by author. Carlsbad, September 2001.

Magazines

"Beach Town after Beach Town on Old 101 north of San Diego" *Sunset Magazine*, September 1981, p. 38.

Carlsbad Resort and Ranch Community. Union Title Insurance and Trust Company, 1952.

Carlsbad Today. Carlsbad Chamber of Commerce, 1979.

Newspapers

Blade Citizen. Oceanside, Calif., 1985–1990.

Carlsbad Free Press. Carlsbad, Calif., April 1952–April 1953.

Carlsbad Journal (Champion). Carlsbad, Calif., 1926–1990.

La Costan. Carlsbad, Calif., April 1982–May 1982.

Spirit of Love. Carlsbad, Calif., 1900–1924.

Other Research

Carlsbad City, Georgina Cole Library. Files at Local History Room.

Carlsbad Historical Society. Files at Magee House Museum.

"Fifty Years of Faith." Saint Patrick's Parish.

ACKNOWLEDGMENTS

I'd like to acknowledge a number of people whose assistance and support made this book possible. My deepest thanks go to Geoff Armour, whose editing skills clarified and enhanced my historical research. His insight and critical advice have been invaluable in creating this book. I also want to thank Marge Howard-Jones, who generously offered her support, time, and historical knowledge to this project. Terri Portner also must be thanked for her energy in reviewing the original manuscript. I would also like to thank all those people who took time from their busy schedules to talk to me. They offered insight into little known or remembered Carlsbad facts and set me off on new areas of research. I thank Bobbie Hoder and Isabel Paulson for their help finding those elusive little facts so necessary to any historical research.

I would like to acknowledge the many hours my husband Germán spent photographing present-day Carlsbad. Needless to say, I thank my husband and sons for their support, understanding, and help completing this project. Without their pushing, prodding, and computer skills this history of Carlsbad would still be untold.

INDEX

D

E

F

G

H

I

J

K

L

M

T

U

V

W

Y

ABOUT THE AUTHOR

Susan Schnebelen Gutierrez is a member of the Carlsbad, San Diego, and Maryland Historical Societies. She is co-author of two historical children's books, co-producer of several historical videos, and editor of a historical cookbook. She lives in Carlsbad with her husband Germán, and sons Chris and Daniel.